D·A·N·C·E

Five Steps to

Living your Best Life

Deborah DeJong, MSW

National Library of Canada Cataloguing in Publication

DeJong, Deborah
    D.A.N.C.E. : five steps to living your best life / Deborah DeJong.

ISBN 1-894933-57-5

    1. Self-help techniques. I. Title.

BF632.D44 2003   158.1   C2003-906025-X

Cover design by hcreates.
Printed and bound in Canada.

Dedication

To my two favourite dance partners,
Spencer and Ashlyn

Acknowledgements

It is with love and appreciation that I acknowledge those people who have been part of my DANCE.

-To all my family and friends who I've shared my life and my dance floor with over the years. Whether you *are* or *were* a part of my life for a reason, a season or a lifetime, I am a better person for having danced with you. Thank you.

-To my parents, their unconditional love and support has always inspired me to live *my* best life. I dance because they showed me how!

-To my clients and participants in my courses, I have learned so much from you and acknowledge your piece in the development of this DANCE model.

-To Chuck McLean, your persistent encouragement and questioning promoted my continued dance with this book. I deeply appreciate and value your support and words of wisdom.

-To Karen Vos Braun, who took my hand and guided me through the literary process. *The Wisdom of Oma* is not only a book you have written, it is your guiding principle to living your best life and supporting those who share the dance floor with you. Thank you for sharing "the wisdom of Karen" and accompanying me on this journey so that others may dance and live their best life.

-To Julie: my sister, my soulmate, my friend (and more recently, my original draft typist). You live the dance! Not only are you the ultimate dancer, you are my biggest fan and for that, I will always be eternally grateful.

You are all dancers to me!

And to everyone who reads this book, I wish you peace and happiness. But above all else, I hope you dance!

D·A·N·C·E
Five Steps to Living Your Best Life

Table of Contents

The DANCE Model

Everything in the universe has rhythm.
Everything dances.
Maya Angelou

Introduction

We each have a unique dance to experience
in living our best life!

*W*elcome to dance class. I am sure many of you know the various steps to the fox trot, the waltz and the polka. Today, we enter into a new realm of dance! A dance for everyone who dares to live their life to the fullest by stepping on to this new dance floor! A dance of the new millenium! A dance in the direction of a new life – full of hope, peace and happiness.

Do you ever feel like you are just going through the motions of life? You get up, go through your daily routines, eating and sleeping? Do you feel like someone else is dragging you across the dance floor? Do you feel like you are not the one in control? Do you feel like you have being doing the same steps for so long that it is inconceivable to start dancing different? This book is for YOU!

How the DANCE model was born

Having worked with individuals, families and groups for over a decade, a few patterns started to emerge that became very telling about an individual's potential for life change and life happiness. The dance floor seemed like a metaphor for life. Some people fall tirelessly, some people are dragged around by others, some people aimlessly crash into others, some people sail. Therefore, this "DANCE" model was born.

The Guiding Principles

The book has been built upon the following four guiding principles.

• Decisions made in the beginning of any life process or event will have the greatest impact on potential outcomes and life happiness. Take the time to make the best decisions possible.

• In order to meet your life goals and care for others you must take care of yourself. You are worth it.

• Spend time with those people who accept and love you unconditionally. Positive people will energize you. Negative people will drain you.

• Listen to your inner wisdom.

These principles form the foundation of the DANCE model. Each chapter was written with these principles in mind as a foundation to support anyone to live their best life.

Why the DANCE model will work for you

The DANCE model is a model designed to change the way you think, behave and make decisions in order to live your best life. It can apply to your personal life, career life, or any of your relationships. It is a step-by-step process to enjoy life more beginning today.

This DANCE model will work for you because it is simple, straightforward and does not require a lot of time on your part. It has been used by many individuals with extreme success and boasts a proven track record. The individual ideas expressed here are not new or novel. The ideas have been with us for years but are now arranged in such a fashion that we can easily remember the steps when we need them most. We DANCE. There is evidence of effective results all around us when we observe the happy and content people in our life. You will be astonished at your own immediate results!

Various life stories will be shared to demonstrate different points throughout the book. Respectfully, names and information have been changed regarding these individuals and their experiences.

How to Use the Book

Often people pick up books and want the "final" answer or "simple quick fix" and fly through the chapters with lightening speed only to be disappointed by the end. Authors often ask questions for readers to ponder and digest, but as readers we simply turn the page and move on. I have come to realize my greatest learning actually took place when I laid the book down and looked deep inside myself to search for the answers and solutions to not only the authors questions but to my own as well. This motivational book is written as though we are having a conversation together. We will look at various concepts in each chapter. Then, I will encourage you to venture out on your own. In order to truly DANCE and take maximum advantage of the dancing process you will need to challenge yourself and go inward to determine which shoes to wear and which musical piece to dance to. For it is *not* the end product of finishing this book that will move your spirit to move, but the dancing process itself on every page that will motivate your DANCE. Avoid hopping from page to page and chapter to chapter to read the words. Instead, dance from page to page and if you are tired, put the book down. When there are questions to consider, let the book sit. There will be moments to "be still" in order to experience the full genius and power of your work and direction of your dance!

Although it may initially appear that the formula for the "DANCE" is very structured or specific, the dance still belongs to *you*. Feel the *rhythm* of your dance in life. The dance is more like a pendulum. You may make a decision, yet hold off on acting on your decision for various reasons. You may decide instead to put your energy into compassion and gratitude before moving back to making decisions. That's okay – move with the flow, even when the winds begin to howl. Believe in yourself. Believe in the Spirit. Believe in your DANCE!

This book should be making suggestions and planting seeds for thought. Take what fits for you and your DANCE and let go of the rest. You may even feel at times "stuck." Put the book down and trust your instincts. Your heart or gut will tell you when it is time to pick up the book again. Remember, only you know what feels right or works for you. Trust yourself – the disc jockey waits for your signal! Be patient. Be kind. Be true. Your frustration may rise if you are rushing into the DANCE only to stumble. Or perhaps after years of dancing the polka you realize that you were meant to be waltzing! At the end of each chapter, there will be room for your personal thoughts and notes to help organize those ideas that have flowed from your spirit while reading. Take the time at the end of each chapter to jot your thoughts and feelings down or to work on the questions and exercises that have been suggested. With these written commitments on the page you will be amazed by the progress which appears in your life. Take time and look back. Reread your thoughts and see where you have been.

It is time to throw caution aside and put your dancing shoes on. They may be dusty but that is irrelevant. It is not the shoes that move a person, but the human spirit that moves the shoes. Come Dance!

Chapter 1

The DANCE Model

"To dare is to lose your footing
momentarily, to NOT dare is to lose
yourself."

Soren Kierkegaard

So what is the answer to eternal bliss and happiness? You must DANCE. That's right! To DANCE is a decision toward change, toward hope, toward what Sarah Ban Breathnach would refer to as "something more." If you choose to DANCE, you will move toward "something more" in your own life.

You will need to set aside your fears and worries and make the decision to move. You will be looking at the DANCE floor of life square in the face claiming "I am ready – Here I come!" Until you make that conscious decision to move and DANCE, life will continue exactly as it is. It may be comfortable, or it may be uncomfortable. Either way, to DANCE will be to leave the familiar behind for something more.

What exactly is the "DANCE" that we are talking about? It is the process by which we make decisions, set goals and strive to attain such dreams in order that we experience the sheer joy of integrity and wisdom. This privilege should not only take place in our final hours, but everyday of our life. Just knowing we are consciously living the DANCE day to day will allow us to experience a sense of integrity and wisdom on a daily basis. This is the process of the DANCE - Your life DANCE.

Components of the DANCE
This process of the DANCE model includes:

> **D** – Decisions
> **A** – Action Plans
> **N** – Navigation
> **C** – Compassion
> **E** – Enjoyment and Evaluation

In Chapter 2, we will be looking at the process of making positive **decisions** in our lives. This is the step where we look at the dance floor and decide what type of DANCE we will be doing – foxtrot, waltz, jazz or limbo. We will determine what your vision for the future truly is, considering various short term, mid term and long term goals. We will address how to enhance your decision making skills to lead your best life.

In Chapter 3, we will be addressing the process of making empowering **action plans**. This is the step where we are actually putting on our dance shoes to prepare for a wonderful life dance. This is where we take our vision for the future and set specific goals. It is the planning process. We will look at the criteria for successful action plans and the "action plan scale" which will guide our goals toward reality. We will consider specific examples of how others have successfully made action plans, as well as issues of caution in this stage.

Chapter 4 is **navigation**. Our shoes have been tied and our decision of which dance we will try has been determined, now we enter the dance floor. This is where we actually start to move on to the dance floor itself. We will learn the key to successful navigation and how to deal with the inevitable setbacks of life. We will also consider how positive self-talk and empowering life affirmations or mantras can have a significant impact on the navigation process.

In Chapter 5, we learn how to navigate the dance floor of life respecting that other people dance with us, around us or beside us. We learn how to dance with **compassion**. We will explore how to practice compassion in our daily lives, as well as why this step is so imperative due to its ripple effects. We will also explore why so many people are held back from compassion because of various fears.

In Chapter 6, we get to close our eyes like trusting children, throw our hair back, flow with the energy set in motion and glide across the floor. We will be **enjoying** the dance. We may take brief "quiet" periods where we open our eyes and **evaluate** where we are and where others are in relation to us, but then the dancing begins again. We will explore how to truly enjoy our lives starting today by using all of our senses. We will also consider what will happen in our life if we do not "stop to smell the roses" and enjoy life. In slowing down to evaluate our dance, we will determine what is working well, what we need to continue doing, what is not working and what changes need to be made to keep dancing.

After all these steps, some people may still feel "stuck" as though they are not making any progress. Often, there is a problem with our dance floor that keeps us from experiencing our best dance. In Chapter 7, we will explore strategies to sweep up or improve our **dance floor**. Maintaining our dance floor is essential to make further progress. We will explore the key to keeping your dance floor clean, smooth and stable. We will also note what to expect if we do not maintain a strong and safe dance floor. Additionally, we will have an opportunity to do a brief test to determine the current strength of our dance floor. Next, we will explore strategies to strengthen our dance floor by looking at our mental, emotional, physical, social and spiritual health.

Some people will not feel "stuck" and may simply want to know how to maintain the integrity of the dance now that they are dancing smoothly over the dance floor. In Chapter 8, we will explore how to maintain your momentum once you are soaring!

How Others Have Used the DANCE Model to Extreme Success

I am sure that you know a "dancer." Someone who makes healthy choices and who generally is calm and confident with strong composure in almost any situation. Think of someone you know who exudes inner peace and contentment. Think about what type of decisions they make. Do you think they spend time planning? Do they dance through life aware of others on their dance floor? Do they dance compassionately? Do you think they take care of themselves (mentally, emotionally, physically, socially, spiritually)? How can you tell?

There are many "dancers" out there. Some "dancers" are our own family and friends. Some "dancers" we recognize through the media. Most of us can identify with a few exceptional "dancers" in particular.

Terry Fox is more than a brilliant demonstration of a true "dancer"; he is a national hero. Terry lost his leg to cancer as a young man, yet he ended up creating the Marathon of Hope to raise money for cancer research. His Marathon of Hope continues in cities across Canada every September. It is obvious that he had a decision to make. He could sit it out or DANCE. Although he probably had many setbacks in his process, it is fair to say he chose the DANCE.

His **decision** to make a difference and raise the awareness of cancer research was made when he decided to run across Canada. He would have had to create various **action plans** before he started on his marathon. His plans would have included when to leave, where to start, who would go with him, sleeping arrangements, media coverage, etc. He started to **navigate** by dipping his toe in the Pacific Ocean and beginning his journey of hope running across Canada on April 20, 1980. He made various stops to speak to crowds, sign autographs and to raise awareness and money for cancer research. His **compassion** was evident throughout his journey as he was aware of the other dancers on the dance floor. He was dancing for them and for a cure for cancer, so that other people would not endure what he had to. There were many moments of laughter and smiles when he was living in the moment and **enjoying** his DANCE (meeting new people on the journey, receiving cheques from various organizations and sharing with friends the events of the day when back in the motor home). Each night he stopped to evaluate the day, the accomplishments, the setbacks and his health. The day arrived when Terry needed to stop his journey to maintain his dance floor. His physical health was depleted and he knew he could not go on. He logged 5,375 kilometres before cancer forced him to abandon his run on September 1 in Thunder Bay, Ontario. His original goal of raising 1 million dollars was far surpassed with contributions to date exceeding 23 million. His DANCE lives on through others. He chose to DANCE.

What about Oprah Winfrey? Not too many people "wing it" to super stardom and ultimate success. She was apparently told early in her career that she would not make it in journalism because her eyes were too far apart. She had a choice to sit it out. Her childhood was of humble beginnings and yet she chose to dream big. She made a conscious choice to DANCE. She had many decisions to make. Her action plans were obviously set in motion and her compassion continues to shine through with the various causes she chooses to support. She has chosen to DANCE.

Some of Terry's and Oprah's choices may not have brought the results they had hoped for, but they always appeared to go back to the start and DANCE again. All of our choices will not be perfect. However, when using this DANCE model your chances of living your best life are greatly enhanced.

The decisions we make today will accumulate to create our life stories. When we make decisions whether regarding how we will live today, how we will live our lives tomorrow or next year, we need to make action plans to set the decisions we have made in motion. When we make specific action plans, there are small steps that need to be addressed to accomplish our goal. Next, we take a leap of faith and go from thoughts to action. In this leap of faith, we navigate our way through the hurdles or setbacks that we face on the dance floor. As we navigate our way over the floor, we must always remember we are sharing this lovely dance space of earth with others. Therefore, we must be aware of and compassionate toward others (people, places and things) so that as we dance we build relationships with people and the environment around us. In dancing compassionately, we will still be able to make a difference and contribute not only to our own goals, but also to the goals of other people around us. Through navigating our way compassionately, we will ultimately have the choice to enjoy each day for what it has to offer. Therefore, the dance of life will have daily doses of wisdom, happiness and joy!

What happens if you do DANCE?

Throughout our lives, we will hear many ideas about how to live our *best life*! Some ideas may be shared by family members. Some may have been learned from strangers or even enemies. Some ideas may have been taught by our neighbour next door. *LIFE LESSONS ARE ALL AROUND US EVERY DAY IF WE ARE OPEN TO OBSERVING THEM.* These opportunities for learning are constantly knocking at our door. We need the right tools and skills to utilize these lessons. It seems that if we do not learn a lesson the first or second time, it comes knocking at our door again. Life lessons come back to us. When in your life did a lesson come knocking and when you chose not to listen, you found yourself in a similar situation down the road? What do you do differently now?

People who choose to DANCE will experience enduring happiness and peace (even when crisis strikes). They will be able to get through the hard times with grace and commitment. They will experience most if not all of the following:

• improved relationships
• enhanced performance

- maximized energy
- personal self wisdom
- enriched vitality
- restful sleep
- reformed responsibility
- internal harmony and external composure
- emotional stability
- positive physical health
- a heightened sense of purpose
- joy, serenity and hope

These are the consequences of dancing! Of course, there are no guarantees that there will be no more pain, but you will possess a new way of looking at your dance and you will have a new set of tools to cope favourably. You will stop blaming others for your misfortunes in life and take ownership for all your life choices (to give power to others for your life disempowers you – you can take it back). You will obtain new skills to assist with all major and minor decision making. You will appreciate that you share this dance floor of life with others and recognize ways to assist and help those in need. You will determine where you are on your DANCE floor of life, what you already know and where you are going. Your new skills will help you start leading your best life today. You will have the formula to authentic living. These are the reasons to DANCE.

If these are not reasons enough, Erik Erikson has researched identity and the life cycle (see Figure 1.1). Erikson wrote that at birth we all go through a variety of developmental stages. At the time of our birth, we will either develop trust or mistrust, based on how our caregivers interact with us. As preschoolers, we develop a sense of autonomy and mastery over life's exercises or we develop shame and doubt (these developments are primarily dependent on how our caregivers or parents dealt with our attempts for independence). We then encounter a stage of feeling proud and secure with our sense of initiative. We confidently try new things, or we perhaps develop a sense of guilt for not "measuring up" to the expectations of others. With a solid sense of initiative, we then move to a state of industry and want to create or build things. This sense of industry helps form our identity in the teen years. Otherwise, a role diffusion or confusion may develop where teens have a greater chance of "following the crowd" into drugs and gangs due to shaky identities or poor refusal skills.

In young adulthood, Erikson spoke of the need for intimacy over isolation, alluding to a continued sense of belonging. In middle adulthood to late adulthood, he refers to the tasks of generativity and/or making a contribution to society versus self-absorption. Erikson suggests that during the adult years, self-absorption ultimately leads to despair and regret versus the wisdom or integrity one may feel of a life well lived in healthy relationships and societal contributions.

In his final stage of identity, "wisdom versus despair," Erikson addresses the question - why dance? In your final hours of life do you want to experience wisdom and integrity or despair?

When I encourage people to dance, some reply, "Why not? I have nothing better to do with my time here on earth

Figure 1.1

Erikson's Stages of Psychosocial Development	Age
Trust vs. Mistrust	Birth to 1-1/2 years
Autonomy vs. Shame and Doubt	1-1/2 to 3 years
Initiative vs. Guilt	3 - 6 years
Industry vs. Inferiority	6 -12 years
Identity vs. Role Confusion	12 - 20 years
Intimacy and Solidarity vs. Isolation	Young Adulthood
Generativity vs. Self-Absorption	Middle Adulthood
Wisdom and Integrity vs. Despair	Late Adulthood

Erikson, E. H. (1980). *Identity and the Life Cycle.*

than to enjoy the dance and this process of life." Others reply that they are quite content to simply exist or go through the motions and let whatever happens just happen. Some people go through life proving themselves to others. They often seem to hold regrets of the past and carry many fears into the future. Their "should have" way of thinking cements them to their past and they spend a great amount of energy trying to control or change others, which only leads to pain and frustration. They may avoid taking risks to avoid further hurt and are constantly concerned about what other people think. They experience little passion for life or self-expression as all their energy is devoted to convincing others and themselves that their appearance of "the perfect life" is really who they are. How exhausting!

In our final hours, sitting in that antique rocking chair slowly swaying back and forth and pondering our life, we will have to answer primarily to one "person" – ourselves! Our choices today will determine if our final tears are tears of sorrow and despair or tears of joy and wisdom.

So why dance? For moments of *joy* today and memories of *wisdom* tomorrow. Do not look back on your life and wonder where your time has gone.

Although Erikson shared his wisdom many years ago, we have great minds among us today with parallel insights. S. Covey, New York Times best-selling author, in the *7 Habits of Highly Effective People,* talks of the need to leave a legacy. We all have a "Fire Within." This need drives us to make certain choices in life - choices to dance! We can all make a difference and leave a legacy. Your DANCE will leave your legacy whether at work, in your family or in your community.

What happens if you do not Dance?

It is simple – prepare for PAIN. Pain in relationships, pain in business, physical pain and potential pain everywhere. Although people view pain differently, it comes down to unpleasant or unwanted feelings. Do you want to live in pain if you have other choices? Some level of stress will always exist, but you will always have the choice to DANCE as a way of dealing with each day.

There are consequences to *all* our choices and decisions. Some consequences are positive (the joy of raising your child) and some consequences are negative (living with lung cancer after years of smoking). The consequence of not dancing is to continue riding the emotional roller coaster you are on, where one day things are fine, the next they are not and so on. You will continue to experience life exactly the way it is now, tomorrow and the next day. If that is okay with you, the DANCE is not for you. Not right now anyway. The

DANCE is for those individuals who want something more in their personal life, at work, and in their relationships!

Most people in pain try to run from it, hide it, deny it, or numb it as a way to cope. They run from one temporary happiness "high" to another happiness "high" without ever truly experiencing true happiness or contentment because when the "high" wears off, the pain returns and they start planning again for another happiness surge. Some people regularly use mind altering recreational drugs or alcohol to numb the pain. Why choose these as your life strategies if there are more effective ways to lasting happiness?

Some painful and challenging issues will arise which are inevitable and you must dance through them or with them (divorce, illness, death, unemployment, etc.) The choice to DANCE is yours once you have the tools at your disposal. The tools are in this book! With these tools you then have the option to dream big!

This next exercise is your opportunity to dream! Imagine the limitless possibilities of your life and where you want to be in two, five, ten or twenty years! What do you see? How do you feel? What do you hear? You must realize that letting your imagination soar can shower many options upon you, but which ones drive you? Perhaps we can have it all, yet we need to start somewhere, where do you want to begin? Which dreams do you choose to focus on?

• Do you want to climb a mountain?
• Do you want to repair a relationship?
• Do you want to witness a sunset in Asia?
• Do you want to sing in a choir?
• Do you want to be part of an Olympic Team?
• Do you want to write a novel?
• Do you want to design a building?

- Do you want to patent an innovative product?
- Do you want to work on a cure for AIDS?
- Do you want to attend school?
- Do you want to learn to play an instrument?
- Do you want to help support children in a third world country?
- Do you want to walk down the aisle of Notre Dame Cathedral?
- Do you want to follow God?
- Do you want to deliver flowers to a hospital?
- Do you want to buy a home?
- Do you want to drive a Hawaiian Orchid Mustang Convertible?
- Do you want to DANCE?

What legacy do you want to leave behind? How will people know you were here? Terry Fox left us the Marathon of Hope. Robin Sharma, author of the national best seller *The Monk Who Sold his Ferrari* is building a library for his children. Will you leave a product? Will you leave a monument? Will you leave a lesson? Oh, the infinite possibilities! What step do we start with in this dance of life? We need to decide!

Let the DANCE begin!

NOTES

_____

_____

_____

_____

_____

_____

_____

_____

_____

_____

_____

_____

_____

_____

_____

_____

_____

_____

_____

_____

_____

_____

Chapter 2
Decisions

The beginning is the most important
part of any work.
Plato

Your Vision

*B*efore we can begin to make decisions for ourselves, we need to clearly consider where it is we want to go and what it is we want for our future. S. Covey suggests in his *7 Habits of Highly Effective People* that we must begin "with the end in mind." Close your eyes for a moment and consider the following questions:

• What do you really want to happen in your life?
• What will be different when you have achieved your goal – when you are "dancing?"
• What will it feel like?
• What will it look like? Can you see the vision?
• What will it smell like or taste like?

Take a minute so that all your senses are congruent with your goal. Before we can dance, we first must decide on which dance we will be doing. If that decision is unclear or foggy, there is a greater probability that we will struggle once we are actually moving on the dance floor. If you have learned the waltz and are ready to perform these steps but then rock music begins to play, you may find yourself in a challenging situation. However, if you decide to waltz and waltz music begins, then you are equipped to successfully meet your dancing goal. The clearer you are with your decisions, the easier it is to plan for and evaluate your outcome. Take the necessary time to be clear with yourself. It will pay off tenfold in the future.

Sitting it Out?

If you are still reading, then there *must* be a passion or dance within you that burns if only by a spark! Keep breathing and adding oxygen. For where there is a spark, there is a flame, and where there is a flame, there is a fire!! *Feed the fire!* Taking time to answer the following questions that appear in this book can actually help you feed your fire. Let me ask you this question. If you decide to let your spark subside, (to put your dancing shoes away), would this decision meet your heart's desire over the long run? Would you be able to look back at your decision to "sit it out" with wisdom *or* with despair? Time is continually in motion and keeps ticking on. There will be multitudes of people who are going to look back on their lives with regret, wondering where time has gone.

Now, that's not to say that some "decisions" can't be put on hold or perhaps are even best on hold for a while. Consciously deciding to wait is not to lose your passion or deny your spirit. It is a decision to "pause" for a while or perhaps focus on a different dance.

There is a significant difference between a "pause" and a "stop." When I decided to travel to Australia to experience new lands, meet new people, taste the Aussie food, sleep under the stars in a swag (insulated sleeping bag) and inhale the salt water swells of the Great Barrier Reef, it was a decision to do my Australian dance (Aussie Dance). Therefore, many other dances went on hold. My writer dance went on pause, because I needed to *live* the stories that I would later write about. My teaching dance also went on pause, for I needed to experience the teachings I would grow from, to empower me as a speaker. You *can* make a decision to put other decisions on hold. Sometimes, it is imperative.

What is even more powerful about your dance lessons is that you have the power (if you decide to act) to move through many dances on any one given day. Therefore, you may consciously decide to make no decisions today or you may be making many decisions about your short term or long term goals. We have been given the precious gift of time. Twenty-four hours a day, 365 days a year – so many decisions to make and dances to dance!

The "Present"

To realize the value of ONE YEAR, ask a student who has failed a grade.

To realize the value of ONE MONTH, ask a mother who gave birth to a premature baby.

To realize the value of ONE WEEK, ask the editor of a week-ly newspaper.

To realize the value of ONE MINUTE, ask the lovers who are waiting to meet.

To realize the value of ONE SECOND, ask the person who just avoided an accident.

To realize the value of ONE MILLISECOND, ask the person who just won silver in the Olympics.

Treasure every moment that you have! Remember that time

waits for no one. Yesterday is history. Tomorrow is a mystery. Today is a gift, that's why we call it "the present."
Author unknown

A decision today can have a profound impact on the rest of your life. Decisions are not just about what you want to do with your life or what you do not want to do. They are also about what you want to get out of the day and what you choose to avoid. Decisions then are like short term and long term goals. Some decisions affect your day (in the short term) and some decisions impact your life (in the long term).

When it comes to decisions, we can break them up into three categories: decisions for the short term (today), for the mid term (this month) and decisions for the long term (years or decades). The following questions will help fuel your fire and build the passion that burns inside. You may be asking the same questions of yourself in the short and long term. If you are feeling stuck, that is fine. Answer the questions that you can and move on. Do not spend your time and energy on "being stuck." Rather, move on to the next question. Some people will experience great challenges with decision making but do not be disheartened. There are many reasons for this situation, which will be addressed later in the book. Do what you can for now and move on.

Decision Making Skills

In *Finding Contentment*, N.C.Warren is quite clear about the importance of consciously processing as many life decisions as you can. He distinguishes between a happiness surge (a quick drink to elevate your mood temporarily or buying a new outfit) and an enduring contentment which lasts a lifetime. His belief is that enduring contentment can only come from being yourself and making *decisions* on your own. You can take the opinions or ideas of others into account, but in the end the decision must be yours.

He invites us to imagine at the centre of our brain a control booth. In the booth are fax machines, phone lines, Internet access and state-of-the-art computer systems. To make good choices we need open communication between our inner wisdom (values, life lessons, feelings) and external sources (significant people in our lives, experts, etc.) He suggests we gather information of what our partner or children may think or want and consider those factors. However, we must also look at our own values and feelings to make the final decision of what we want. *We* make the decision or else we give our power away and contentment or true authentic living may not appear in our lives. A woman named Mary Anne once told me she made *no* decisions and that every decision was made for her child. Mary Anne's female friends were doing a "girls day" of shopping but she could not go since her daughter had a soccer tournament. As we got talking, it became clear that Mary Anne had taken her child's needs into account but she had also been in her control booth. Mary Anne had carefully considered her personal values (family, positive parenting) and her own feelings (she knew her daughter Susan would not always want her at the games and she wanted to savour these moments as long as she could). In the end, *Mary Anne* still made the decision to go to the tournament. It's never too late to make positive decisions using this model of identifying data or information from various sources, listening to them within the frame of your own values and feelings and following through. Decision making skills can be learned at a young age or at any time in life. These skills have the greatest long term impact on authentic living so it is wise to invest some time and energy into learning them and sharing them.

The Questions
Short term:
What do you want to do today?

_____

What do you want to accomplish or experience this week?

_____

Where do you need to go?

_____

Who do you need to connect with?

_____

What minor steps need to be taken?

_____

What can you do to address your Mental Health? Emotional Health? Physical Health? Social Health? Spiritual Health?

_____

_____

_____

Mid term:
What do you want to do for your next vacation?

_____

What do you hope to accomplish at school or at home?

_____

What do you want to accomplish at your present job?

_____

Who do you need to visit?

_____

What do you hope to be doing next year at this time?

_____

Where would you like to travel on a day trip?

_____

Long term:
What do you hope to be doing in five years?

_____

What do you hope to be doing in ten or twenty years?

_____

What do you hope to know?

_____

What information or knowledge do you hope to have?

_____

Where do you hope to work?

_____

What will your position be?

_____

Where would you like to travel? (overnight holidays or vacations)

_____

When would you like to travel there?

_____

What sites would you like to see?

_____

Where would you like to live? When would you like to live there?

_____

What kind of dwelling would you like to live in?

_____

Who will be part of your life?

_____

Who would you like to become?

_____

What do you want to remember out of life in your final hours?

_____

None of these aspirations or dreams will come true if you don't make conscious choices or decisions to move in those directions. Your decisions may change over time, which is perfectly fine! We are all human and we make mistakes and hopefully learn from them and grow. We also have the *right* to change our minds. A decision today may change completely or simply go on the back burner for awhile, when other more urgent or important decisions need to be addressed.

Dawn's Story: Short term effects of decision making

I remember working with Dawn one day who felt she had many issues on her plate and she struggled to make simple decisions. She had just been told her eldest of four sons would need to be in vocational school until age 21. Then he was to move on to a group home setting, as he would never be able to take care of himself. Her hopes and dreams for her baby to grow up and have a rewarding job, a loving wife and healthy children had just been squashed. All she had ever wanted for her son was happiness. Since he was regularly taunted and led astray by bullies at school and in the community, she saw little hope in his future. Five professionals sat around a massive board table that day and told her that her son's life dreams were limited. The message she received was that his hopes and dreams were impossible. Her other son needed extensive dental work and the bills had started to build. Her youngest son had been on a waiting list to see a developmental pediatrician for more than a year. When the appointment came, she was told he needed medication for attentional and learning difficulties. All four boys had learning difficulties and were on modified school programs. On top of all this, her migraines continued on a daily basis. Sometimes her medication helped with her depression but other days it did not seem to make a difference. Her ex-husband continued to remind her that her parenting skills were reportedly "pathetic." I asked her who her supports and friends in her life were and she could not think of anyone. Her family seemed to judge her for not having a job, yet it is challenging to find work when you cannot read or write. She felt alone, scared and hopeless.

In the past, she would have decided to deal with the news regarding her son's future by retreating to her room and sleeping – for hours and even days. She admitted she often found it easier to "sit it out!" But today, even with the harsh words of her son's reality upon her, she had a choice to sit it out (go back to bed) or DANCE (make a decision to address her social, emotional or physical needs). And today, she chose to DANCE.

One of Dawn's neighbours had recently received some negative medical news and needed some company. Dawn made a (short term) *decision* to walk over to her neighbours for a lukewarm tea. They sat at a picnic table enjoying companionship in the April sunshine. Not many words were spoken as they both chose to avoid talking of their inner troubles. Instead, they shared words of encouragement and kindness. In taking care of her social (companionship with a trusted neighbour) and emotional needs (sharing some of her feelings), she chose to dance! This *decision* was a small step toward happier moments that she may not have foreseen that day. In taking care of herself and getting outside, she broke a cycle of retreat that had existed for months. Dawn felt proud of herself for making the decision and taking the step. Therefore, she appeared happier when her boys returned home from school that day. There were less arguments vying for their mother's attention. They were getting along better as a family which created more positive energy in the house, as opposed to the past hostile energy. Since the boys felt better about themselves, when bullies approached them the next day at school, they were less reactive and stronger in utilizing the social skills they had been taught. When the bullies did not get the reaction they expected, they moved on. The eldest boy, with new found confidence, made a new friend and invited him home. He had not brought a classmate home in over a year. This positive cycle was started with a decision to go out for tea and DANCE. Small decisions today can lead to bigger success stories tomorrow if you just *decide* to dance.

Therefore, by breaking down our decisions into short, mid and long term segments, we do not need to be overwhelmed with huge long term or life choices. Sometimes our small decisions provide us with smaller success stories and confidence that we can build upon to get us where we truly want to go in life. Children do not get up and start running right away. First, there is falling and wobbling before learning to walk. We all need to take baby steps before we take off running. Do not forget to focus on your short term goals just as much, or *more* than your long term goals. Then, remember to reward yourself for doing these short term goals for they build your future and you want to enjoy the process along the way.

If writing these goals down is not for you, be creative. Use pictures. Draw them yourself or cut them out of magazines. If you have a short term goal to go to the park today, then draw a picture of a park. If you have a mid term goal to buy a new car, cut out a picture from a magazine and mount it on your fridge or somewhere where you will see it often. If you have a long term goal to build a log cabin, find yourself a picture and post it as a regular reminder.

Why should we put so much time and energy into making these decisions? Because decisions made early on have the greatest impact on living your best life. Do not let others determine when you sit it out, since only you have control of *your* decisions and emotions. Events may come your way that are out of your control but you can still decide how to deal with them.

A Story of Two Sisters:
Long term effects of decision making

In a small rural area of southern Ontario, a mother called to her eldest daughter, "Let's go! Do you have your shoes?!" A spirited young six-year-old came hustling out of her bedroom elated with energy. Tonight was dance class and they were learning a new step! Her mother could not drive fast enough to the dance studio where she took lessons with six other girls her age. She flew up the stairs and threw on her shoes leaving her mother somewhere in the dust. She could not *wait* to dance. It was in her blood!

The class began as usual and the step tonight was a bit tricky. All the mothers watched in their row of chairs behind the dancers. The music was speeding up and this young girl's spirit kept pace. She put her whole body into the dance that night and over-exaggerated her steps to truly *feel* the music and let the music live through her. She no longer was moving step, shuffle, hop. She was truly experiencing the dance of life and simply enjoying being alive!

With energy that intense and allowing herself to "let go," she became less aware of her surroundings. Her eyes closed and her body relaxed. She experienced then, the unthinkable. With a shoelace untied and oblivious to what could happen, she lost her footing and fell flat on her back. Her dance was literally over within a second! Just like that. The music stopped. Her eyes opened, she looked up, and the other girls helped her up. With nothing injured but her pride she went off to sit by her mother (to sit the next dance out). The next song started and still she remained glued to her mother. The embarrassment was too much for a six-year-old to bear. One song played and then another. Her mother was losing patience, but the young girl adamantly refused to rejoin the dance class.

She held back stubborn tears as she literally hid behind her mother's chair. The other girls would glance over with smiles of encouragement and yet the inner pains of humiliation would not allow this little dancer's feet to move. The longer she waited, the harder it became to return to the dance class. She remained behind that chair and simply observed the dance floor and the other dancers. Even though she desperately wanted that feeling back, her pride held her back. One fall and the dance was over! This dancer took off her shoes that night and never put them back on. She chose to sit it out.

Some years later, that dusty and rusty pair of shoes were resurrected from the closet of that young dancer's home. Her mother shined them up and handed them to her younger sister. Off to class this new young dancer went. All excited to learn the new steps and diligent to practice at home. In any true dancer's life, we must know there will come that moment known as *"the fall!"* That moment came. When it did, history had the potential to repeat itself in the life of this younger sibling. But it did not!

This vibrant younger sibling fell during class, brushed herself off and jumped right back up. She fell during practice, and got back up! Dance floors can be slippery and sure enough during a recital, this little spirited dancer fell, and yet, got back up! Numerous family and friends watched embarrassed *for* her but admired her sense of adventure, commitment and discipline. It takes more than desire to dance. Desire is fleeting. It takes more than determination to dance. We all will get tired. It takes *discipline*. This dancer was disciplined!

Then, one day while representing Canada she did not just fall – she fell clear off the stage! If there ever was a moment for a decision to dance or not to dance, this would have been it! What do you suppose this young dancer did? She chose to DANCE! She made a conscious decision to get back up and dance. She danced on to become a five time Canadian Open Group Stepdance Champion with her entourage, *The Rainbow Connection!* She continues to teach dance classes and judge at national competitions. She truly continues to DANCE!

This inspirational dancer is my sister Julie! It is an honour to share her good news and spirit with others. She is an inspiration and positive role model of integrity and of the human spirit to many people. With every reason or excuse to give up, she kept dancing and now continues to give her best in everything she does!

What happened to the other dancer? Well, here I am! Every time I see her numerous trophies throughout our parents' home, it reminds me that life is precious and that we won't be here forever. We all need to make decisions today about how we plan on spending the rest of our lives. Our smaller daily decisions affect our life decisions. Therefore, we need to be aware of our daily, monthly and yearly choices because they have the power to affect our lives in a very powerful way. Will you sit it out, or DANCE? I dance more often than I sit it out these days! I hope you will choose to DANCE too!

The Element of Change

Our decisions, then, have the power to change our lives. In reading about leadership wisdom in *The Monk Who Sold His Ferrari*, Robin Sharma writes about a principle to enhance your dance: surrendering to change. If you are excited to dance gracefully and soulfully through your journey of life, then it is fair to say that change is a given. It is inevitable and should be welcomed like a fresh new beginning or a sunrise every morning. Beware, because change (even positive change) has it's costs and struggles.

Change can be positive and negative all at once! We need to surrender to change, accept it and embrace it. Be easy on yourself, for change is not easy. How will you embrace the changes of your dance? What messages will help you sustain a hopeful attitude? Perhaps these affirmations can assist you during periods of change.

• I can do this!
• I've been through worse. I can get through this!
• I am in control!
• I have power!

Who will be your support network – those empowering voices to encourage you (friends, family, colleagues, neighbours, children, or relatives)?

In the beginning stages of the DANCE, making decisions and experiencing some changes will be difficult. You may need to make the toughest decisions of your life, but perhaps also your best decisions. Take heart! The *decision* to dance may be your finest hour!

NOTES

_____

_____

_____

_____

_____

_____

_____

_____

_____

_____

_____

_____

_____

_____

_____

_____

_____

_____

_____

_____

_____

_____

Chapter 3
Action Plans
Putting Our Dancing Shoes On

"I am the master of my fate;
I am the captain of my soul."
William Ernest Henley

*F*irst – the Decision to Dance. Then – our Action Plans which will take us there!

If you are reading this book, it would seem the first decision has already been made. You choose to DANCE! There may be many reasons for this choice. You may be tired of feeling negative, or tired of the comfort of the status quo. You may be restless or agitated. You may be feeling stuck. You may be feeling temporarily satisfied or joyful and want to project this feeling into your future. You may want to make a difference for yourself and others, yet maybe you do not know where to start. You may simply want to smile more.

Whatever brings you here - welcome. You now have a bigger task regarding the planning and direction of your DANCE!

Goal Setting

We are *all* goal setters. We are constantly making decisions every day, although we hardly are aware of it. Some of us may plan our days more precisely than others.

We may make a daily list that sets our goals and maps our day. The map may begin with a shower, breakfast, or preparing lunches. We may continue with making certain calls before break, attending a late morning meeting, meeting a friend for lunch, taking a quick walk, and spending time on a project. It may continue with picking up groceries, making supper, and reading the paper before heading to bed.

If you can organize your thoughts (written or in memory), then you can plan your day. If you can plan your day, then you can plan your year. If you can plan your year, then you can plan your life. If you can plan your life, you can DANCE!

The only real difference between planning your day and planning your life is time and investment. Planning your life will obviously take more time, thought and investment. Your daily maps are short-term. We are still not moving on the dance floor, but we are mapping which direction we will go and the details needed to get there.

Some people insist they are not "planners," they like to follow and just "go with the flow." When I ask them if they use a day planner they say "of course." When I ask if they ever make lists (written or mental) for work purposes or personal reasons (a grocery list) they often reply, "yes." Then I tell them, "you are a planner!" We are *all* planners! We just use different life maps and plan in different ways. Get out your pen, markers, paints or palm pilots and create your map!

Start with your day. Some people break it up by the hour or three time chunks of morning, afternoon and night. Remember, you will achieve your best results the more *specific* you are. Take your time and be patient with yourself. This exercise may come quite easily to some people because it is a daily habit. It may be more challenging for others, but with challenge comes fulfillment. It is important to incorporate the five components of self-care (mental, emotional, physical, social and spiritual health) into your plans. We will look at these components in greater detail in Chapter 7. A sample day may look something like this:

Morning	- breakfast
	- schedule a doctor appointment
Afternoon	- walk in park for lunch
	- explore a new product line on Internet
	- send out resume
	- errands (bank, drycleaners)
	- prepare supper
Night	- physical activity (gym, jog, basketball)
	- call a friend
	- date with partner or friend
	- read a favourite book

Once you have your daily list or map, star those items that are most important to achieve. In their book *First Things First*, S. Covey and R. Merrill refer to this idea as prioritizing so that you are sure to accomplish those things that truly matter most today. If you do not prioritize, you may suffer the pain of letting the "little" things control your life.

Once you have spent some time practicing daily maps, you can start planning your life map. This is simply a map, so if you have a choice in the beginning to practice planning big or planning small, go big!

Put every detail you can into that map just for the practice. Practice leads to positive progress and we are talking about your life. When looking at dance maps (or life maps) some people choose to go by years. Others go by decades or by months. Life maps look at your goals over time, which is very important. Remember the questions in Chapter 2? Remember the answers you came up with?

• Where do you want to be in five, ten, or twenty years?
• What do you want to be doing?
• Who do you want to know?
• Where do you want to live?
• What do you want to have accomplished?
• Where do you hope to have been?

These lifetime dreams will help you determine your DANCE. If you lose sight of these values, you will continue surviving in life instead of thriving! Once these lifetime dance goals are clearer, it is easier to focus on the present! How do we dance now? How do we plan further along with the *specifics* to meet our lifetime DANCE goals?

What if we don't know exactly what we want in five or ten or twenty years? Not to worry, most of us don't. Even if we have a general idea, this will be helpful. If you have no idea, you can still dance today. We will come back to this issue later (Chapter 7). For those who have an idea of their dance, this action planning step is imperative to clarify long term dreams and to assist with short-term goals. Although this step of making specific action plans may seem trivial or unnecessary on the surface, it is very important. It helps clarify your goals in the short term. It helps with organizational and adaptability skills which are essential in the long term.

Criteria for Action Plans

Here we face the dance floor, looking it right in the eye. We have made a decision. We know what we want and now must secure a strong action plan to ensure we get where we choose to go. This action planning is like the final steps of putting on your shoes and tying them up before actually going out on the dance floor.

There are ten guidelines that will help in the action planning stage. After they are listed, we will explore them in more detail.

1 – Be specific.
2 – Be realistic.
3 –*You* have the power of choice. (Avoid letting others make your decisions for you).
4 – Use positive language. (Language is powerful).
5 – Word your end goal in the present tense.
6 – Practice patience, perseverance and persistence – not procrastination.
7 – Beware of your goals that are based on the wishes or desires of others.
8 – Recognize *all* aspects of the goal accomplishment.
9 – Incorporate Supreme Self-Care.
10 – Have *fun!*

Let's explore these further.

1. Be Specific!

The more specific and clear we are, the easier it is to measure and evaluate progress, outcomes and accomplishments. Vague planning leads to vague results, specific planning leads to specific results.

Sarah made a plan to get "a job." Because she was not specific in the type of job (the hours she hoped to work, the pay scale, etc.), she got a job but the job was not suited for her or her needs. Sarah was miserable. The job took her down a path that actually led her away from, instead of toward, her long term dreams. If she had spent more time initially being specific about what she hoped to gain, her life satisfaction would have been different.

2. Be Realistic

Realistic goals are ones that you can truly see yourself living or dancing! Unrealistic goals, although perhaps idealistic, are goals that really do not fit for you or your lifestyle. These goals often are imposed on you by others (family, friends, children, or society itself). It may seem noble to want to cure cancer, however, if you have no medical or research training it would be unrealistic and self-defeating to pursue such a goal without considerable re-direction around schooling. I am not suggesting you dream small, but realistically big! Continue to ask yourself and others – what will it take to make this dream possible?

3. *You* have the power of choice

Sometimes it is easier to let others make your decisions and in the end they may be happy – but will you? No one else can define your happiness. Happiness ultimately comes from understanding how to dance and enjoy life. If you let others make your choices (a parent, spouse, child), you give up your right and freedom to choose which ultimately will lead to something less than your complete definition of utopia. Remember who is in your control booth.

4. Use Positive Language

Words are very powerful, so make sure to use positive and affirmative language.

"I am smoke free" versus "I want to quit smoking."

"I am employed" versus "I am not unemployed."

"I am married to a kind and compassionate partner" versus "I am no longer alone."

5. Work Your End Goal in the Present Tense

We want to speak to ourselves (internally) as though the goal is already accomplished and in place.

"I am married" versus "I will be married."

"I accept my space at college" versus "I will go to college."

"I am healthy" versus "I am no longer sick."

These statements are not meant to be shared with others. They are meant to be said internally and to strengthen your commitment.

6. Practice Patience, Perseverance and Persistence

These three P's will assist in action planning or mapping by eliminating excuses or interruptions to achieving your short or long-term plans. They will help you focus and avoid distractions. There will always be opportunities to avoid planning by ignoring your decisions to dance. A friend may call and ask you over for coffee, or your boss may ask you to do an extra shift. If you have committed to an evening of "planning" then "plan!" Be persistent about your need to persevere. However, if an emergency arises (and you know what the difference is), be patient with yourself and the situation. Avoid giving up all together. Schedule planning for a different time on a different night. Do persevere. Do persist. These elements are the difference between an unknown genius and a well-known genius.

7. Beware of Your Goals that are Based on the Wishes or Desires of Others

Some people set goals by comparing their lives to others. Although it may seem harmless on the surface, goals based on envy, greed or jealousy have a way of torturing us and not bringing us fulfillment because they are not ours. They are not authentic. They belong to someone else.

It may seem that if we only had a million dollars, or if we were a celebrity on television or a neighbour down the street, we would be much happier. However, money does not bring happiness. It may bring a sense of financial security or comfort perhaps, but there are other strategies to obtain these feelings. Just ask someone who has money if they are always "happy" and you will be surprised at the issues they face. In the end, only you know what is truly important for you. Listen to your own heart, not to others or you will be disappointed. You should always be asking yourself "do I really, really want this?" On a scale of 1 to 10 (1 being "not really" and 10 being "totally") how badly do you want this goal? If your answer is 5 or lower, perhaps it is not truly your desire but the desire of someone else.

8. Be Careful What You Plan For

The old saying suggests "be careful what you wish for, it may just happen." This is true. When looking at your action plans and maps you need to look at *all* aspects of the goal. If you truly are planning for optimal health, you may need to be prepared to give up your disability cheque. If you are planning to have a full-time job, this may ultimately mean less time for family and friends. Be aware of what your goals will bring (both positive and negative). All decisions have natural or logical consequences. You will need to look at the pros and cons of your decisions since both exist. What are the benefits to your decision? What are the consequences? Can you live with the balance? Is this decision one you really want to act on at this time?

9. Incorporate Supreme Self-Care

Throughout your planning stage, make sure to keep in mind the constant necessity to take care of yourself and maintain a sturdy dance floor. Without a strong physical, mental, and emotional inner foundation, dancing becomes impossible if not treacherous and perhaps even dangerous. Therefore, when looking at your life map, how are you meeting your mental, emotional, physical, social and spiritual needs? When planning a daily map, does it address these five components? It is important that in all planning and regular mapping, these issues are constantly being addressed or you will not be able to truly enjoy the dance. We will explore this issue further in Chapter 7.

10. Have FUN!

The action planning part of the DANCE is meant to be fun and adventurous. We will start some real work in the navigation stage, but for now, let your planning be fun. We all have a need to laugh and enjoy life and although we may be trying to find specific and positive goal language – have *fun*! Happiness is not only the pot of gold at the end of the rainbow, it is the rainbow. Enjoy the process of the whole dance including the planning stage. *You* know what fun means.

Let's look more closely at the pre-action planning stage.

Pre-Action Planning Stage

Now we plan by narrowing down our dance to a smaller time frame. For example, if we know we want to retire at fifty-five, what financial planning or investing do we have to address in our twenties, thirties or forties to achieve that goal? If you are not currently working, then your dance plan may be focused at this point on securing a job. If you are considering going back to school, you may need to do some research on the best programs, your true interests, relocation issues, and financing.

This stage of action planning is focused on bringing the bigger picture down to size and planning how your DANCE might look step-by-step. You may find it helpful to have two or three action maps dealing with various life goals (one for your personal life, family life, and career life). The greater detail you put into your maps, the greater chance of success you have (even if modifications need to be made).

Speaking of modifications, these are part of life. They are part of planning and they are part of the DANCE. How many people build a house and stick *precisely* to the original plan? How many people start a business with a mental map or idea in mind and stick *exactly* to the original vision? How many people create a new garden and do not allow room for something unique or colorful that was not on the original plan? Very few. When you are building or creating something special, you need to be flexible. Be prepared to make modifications throughout your life. This is simply part of planning, since the only constant in life is change! It is much harder to maintain optimal self-care if you are rigid or "stuck" on every aspect of your plan. Adaptability, flexibility and integrity are crucial for action plans.

The Action Plan Scale

Now that you have your goal in mind and have phrased it in positive affirming language in the present tense, (i.e. "I am employed full-time"), you are going to use scales to assist you in making progress towards that goal. You are going to focus on detail since it is detail that will ultimately assist you to identify small elements of progress. It is important to remember we are not focussing on your goal being perfectly met, we are focussing on progress and the smaller necessary steps that move you along the scale towards your goal.

Your scale will be a continuum between 1 and 10:
1…..2…..3…..4…..5…..6…..7…..8…..9…..10

1 will be the absence of your goal.
10 will be the presence of your goal.

For example:

Renting 1 --- 10 Owning

Depressed 1--10 Happy

Unemployed 1 -------------------------------------10 Employed

Many Panic Attacks 1 -------------------10 Few Panic Attacks

Therefore, we are always trying to climb towards the 10 (not descending or moving down when it comes to life planning). We need to use powerful positive language when progressing in our life planning. Each individual will need to spend considerable time filling in 2 to 9 with mini tasks that lead towards their final goal. This is **action planning**.

Let us look at an example of an unemployed, skilled person wanting to obtain work in their area of expertise. On the scale, 10 would be "working full time" and 1 would be "not working." There are many steps an unemployed person may take to move toward employment. There are no right or wrong answers here regarding what 2 versus 3 may be. What may be a 2 on one person's scale may be a 5 on another. Resist the urge to compare. Comparing will only feed the mind of envy or jealousy and that is not what strengthens your dance.

Using the example of an unemployed person, what might they do to get to 2 or 3 or 4?

1 - Unemployed
   - No prospects
   - No efforts made in phone contacts
2 - Buy a newspaper
3 - Circle possible job opportunities (remembering skills, hours available, etc.)
4 - Prepare resume, inform friends/family of intentions
5 - Make 2 inquiry phone calls
6 - E-mail, send or drop off resume to "Company Z"
7 - Record dates/times/contacts/locations where resumes were sent
   - Prepare for interviews (practice mock interviews with a friend)
8 - Attend interviews
9 - Make follow up phone calls
   - Enquire as to how to improve for future interviews
10- Accept a full-time position

OR

1 - Not currently working
2 - Go for walk in area where you want employment (Observing help wanted signs)
3 - Fill out application
4 - Speak to others who work there, find out how they were hired
5 - Make follow up calls where you completed applications
6 - Prepare resumes, print off 25 resumes, buy stamps
7 - Research who to send cover letter to, prepare cover letter
8 - Drop off resumes to contact person or e-mail them directly
9 - Follow up phone call, prepare for interview
10 - Accept position

You can see that one scale is very different than the other. The more specific you can be, the better. This example does not suggest the best ten steps to employment. It only demonstrates the significance of specific steps one must take to work towards a goal.

Some people may choose to have two or three specific tasks before moving from four to five. Your level 6 may have four points included and level 7 only one point. That is okay. You do not necessarily need only one point each time. Some people may prefer to write their scale horizontally across the page instead of vertically. Some people may choose to write their action plan in the form of ten steps ascending to their goal. Ten rungs on a ladder climbing to the top of their goal is another popular way of mapping goals.

Some authors like S. Covey and C. Richardson suggest putting time limits with each step to encourage persistence and keep you on task. This element of time is totally your choice.

Precautions

When it comes to our action plans, we need to be cautious about a few things. One significant issue is communication with others. Some theorists like Wayne Dyer, author of *Manifest Your Destiny*, may suggest that mental and spiritual planning be kept to ourselves in our heads and in our hearts with an internal trust or "confident knowing" that things will work out. Dyer believes we do not need to tell others about our plans because they will manifest or happen in our lives over time anyway. He suggests it is simply our "ego" telling others of our plans instead of trusting our intuition.

Other theorists like Anthony Robbins, author of *Awaken the Giant Within*, would suggest we share our plans with family and friends because this commits us to our plans even more. If we are somehow sharing our dreams or goals with others, we are making a verbal commitment to them and to the world. If others are aware of our intentions, we may feel more motivated. We might say to ourselves, "I better work on this project since other people know!"

When it comes to open communication, my best recommendation is to practice discretion and balance. When you choose to share your "dance" with others – use discretion in deciding who you share it with. Someone you have known for quite a long time, or someone who will support you emotionally and mentally may be appropriate. Someone who is trustworthy and will not share with their partner or colleague or someone who will be there for you even if your goal is never achieved may be worthy of your trust and dreams.

Sometimes we share our dreams with the wrong person and we learn the hard way who to trust. Therefore, look for a balance when sharing goals or holding them close to your heart. With modifications, plans *do* change, so sharing initial goals with others may appear as though you have difficulty following through. Others may criticize or talk behind your back about your "idealistic expectations." That kind of non-supportive gossip says more about them (and their unstable dance floor) than it does about you and your desire to dance! Do not own their issues and do not let their negativity or fear swallow your passion for your DANCE! If *they* choose not to dance, all the more room on the dance floor for you!

Here we are! We have decided on some potential life plans and mapped out our action plans for our DANCE. Our lists are made, our scales are in place and the next stage of our dance has arrived. We have put our dance shoes on, laced them up and approached the dance floor with eyes wide open and bright with passion. Now, as we stand before our dance floor with excitement, anxiety and intrigue it is truly time to move and "Navigate" the DANCE!

Chin up. Shoulders back. Smile. Let's DANCE!

NOTES

Chapter 4
Navigation
Stepping on to the Dance Floor

We will be known by the tracks we leave behind.
Dakota Proverb

Now, it is time to act and to move! We have decided the time is right for movement and change. We know what needs to be done to move us towards our dreams. We have envisioned our goal and have made a conscious action plan to realize our dreams. We have put our dancing shoes on and are now looking straight at the dance floor. In essence, a moment of truth.

Our shoes may feel too tight at first or not our proper size. That is okay. It is part of the dance. We may need to experiment with many types of shoes (sneakers, pumps, docs, workboots, sandals, etc.) and many sizes (1 – 18). It is the process of the dance itself where the reward lives and finding the shoes that will magically fit us.

We all know people who have big plans in life, big dreams they share but somehow they just don't seem to happen. We also know there have been times in our own lives when plans we had just did not happen for various reasons. Perhaps someone else's plans changed our plans, or something beyond our control took place. Perhaps we did not put forth the effort to make our plans a reality. Here we are again, plans in place, but what happens now? It is the test!

Your test!

It is in *navigating* across the dance floor where most people get "stuck" or choose to run safely to the sidelines for stability. Our aspirations and dreams can be so overwhelming; so passionate. It is one thing to create an action plan in our head, but it is quite another to put those action plans into motion. Here we stand, at the edge of the dance floor wanting to move forward, wanting to dance! Our shoes are tied, the music has started and with a big deep breath we take our first step (and the first step is the hardest).

This spot is where we pick up our action map or plan and move from "mental" practice to "physical" practice. We actually do what we have mapped out. We pick up our scale having determined where we currently are (2/10 or 4/10 or 7/10), and we actually *do* what we believe is required to get to the next step.

You actually may be doing one or many of the following, depending on your goal:

- making (a phone call)
- calling (a friend)
- buying (a ticket)
- visiting (a customer)
- sending (an e-mail)
- delivering (a letter)
- registering (for a course)
- attending (a class)
- listening (to a colleague)
- speaking (to an employer)
- problem solving (with a neighbour)
- connecting (with a loved one)
- arranging (a meeting)

- writing (a letter)
- joining (a fitness centre)
- typing (a note)
- walking (a mile)
- organizing (your desk)
- acting (on a message)

R. Sharma (1997: p.115), in *The Monk who Sold His Ferrari*, speaks of the importance of applying ourselves if change is to take place. He states, "most people know what they should do in any given situation, or in their lives for that matter. The problem is that they don't take daily consistent action to apply the knowledge and realize their dreams." The same is true with our DANCE. It is one thing to "decide" to eat more healthy, it is another thing to actually *do* it.

A Story of Successful Navigation

A young woman, Cindy, was diagnosed with cancer early in her life. She was twenty-seven. From the beginning, she made a conscious decision that she was going to DANCE. She decided she would get second opinions from doctors and follow the consensus of their best advice. Her action plans included:

- Taking the prescribed medications (morning, noon and night)
- Keeping a physical activity routine (weights - Monday, Wednesday, Friday, and aerobic activity -Tuesday, Thursday, Sunday)
- Making sure her diet included the recommended servings of each food group
- Attending all doctor appointments

- Taking a leave of absence from work
- Scheduling surgery as soon as possible
- Attending all treatment schedules (chemotherapy, radiation)
- Phoning one friend daily to touch base and obtain support
- Inquiring about personal counselling
- Booking regular massages

She had quite the detailed plans! However, it was not an action plan that saw her regain total health. It was how she navigated through the dance that made all the difference. That commitment and perseverance to remain dancing when it would have been easier to leave the dance floor made all the difference. It would have been easier to continue grabbing fast food at lunch or sitting on the couch watching soap operas instead of calling a friend, going to the gym or keeping appointments. She literally pushed herself to her appointments. Cindy did not just "talk the talk" regarding her action plans. She truly "walked the walk" which is the hardest part of the DANCE! We all are human and will feel the pains of self-defeat or of not wanting to move on. That is normal. You will be okay. Regroup and reward yourself as you get yourself back on your original path or plan.

The Key to Navigation
You will need to return to your action map regularly to determine what you have accomplished and where you need to go. Now, for every step you have taken on your action map, you need to *reward your effort* (even if nothing came of your attempt)! This self-reward is the key to successful navigation toward making your dreams come true. It is easy to get discouraged when we have worked hard to make progress in a certain direction of our life and nothing seems

to be changing. Sometimes, positive progress occurs, but it is beyond what the visual eye can see or the heart can understand. Perhaps there are good reasons why certain action plans do not develop as planned, and one day we will be able to look back and smile in gratefulness for our unanswered prayers. The more discouraged or defeated you feel the more imperative it is to focus on baby steps of progress and rewarding yourself often. You are worth it!

Keep in mind, if you keep changing your decisions or action plans, it becomes more challenging to navigate and to truly enjoy the dance. Although you may continue to recognize small steps of progress and you may continue giving yourself daily self-rewards, you are never actually accomplishing any one particular goal or decision. You may not be "stuck" but you may be starting to spin! Some people start to witness these patterns in their lives and we will discuss how to deal with these patterns in Chapter 7.

Self Reward

"What *is* self-reward," you might ask. It is rewarding yourself for even small steps in the right direction. That is correct, *you are going to acknowledge and reward all steps taken towards your destination or goal.*

It will obviously be quite important to decide in advance what your rewards are. What small things can you do for yourself to pat yourself on the back and say, "Way to go!"

This exercise can be a fun exercise, so enjoy it. Take a few minutes to randomly jot down fifty ways you could reward yourself. A sample list may include:

-watching a favourite movie -reading a favourite poem
-looking at a photo album   -picking a rose from your garden

-calling an old friend
-visiting a library/museum
-taking a scented bath
-buying flavoured coffee
-sleeping in
-eating chocolate
-hugging a loved one
-biking in the woods
-getting a massage
-caressing a pet
-nestling up with a book
-writing a letter
-cuddling
-watching the stars
-holding a baby
-people-watching at the park
-feeding the birds/ducks
-enjoying sun on your face
-breathing fresh air
-ordering in food

-wearing your favourite outfit
-painting your nails
-having a strawberry milkshake
-enjoying a hammock ride
-listening to a favourite cd
-visiting a favourite place
-spraying a scent on your pillow
-getting a new haircut
-eating fresh tomatoes
-going for a country drive
-taking an extra long shower
-going on a day trip
-golfing
-playing poker with the "boys"
-going for a motorcycle ride
-taking an extra nap
-playing a video game
-getting a pedicure
-reading the newspaper
-deep breathing

Note: These self-rewards are *not* about money. Some of these self-rewards may have a price attached but most of them should be pure simple pleasures. They should also be within your control (for example, going for a walk versus *receiving* a letter from an old friend). Although receiving a letter may be a reward, it is a reward from someone else, not yourself. Your rewards must come from you! Re-reading the letter may be a self-reward.

If you jot down fifty small rewards and still have free-flowing ideas, keep going. Keep writing. Don't stop until your list is completely exhausted. Remember, your list may grow or change from day to day. What *once* was a reward may change. For example, calling a certain friend for a chat may have been a reward until a conflict arose or they moved away and phone calls got fairly expensive and e-mail lost the personal touch. Review your list often and add or delete as you wish. No one can define a self-reward for you but *you!*

If it is difficult for you to make a list, get the help of a trusted friend. Perhaps they can write and you can just brainstorm out loud for a while. They may have suggestions of what they believe you may enjoy but only you can decide if it is a personal reward to put on your list. You decide if it is truly you. Start with five or six ideas. Five or six ideas are a good starting point. As ideas come to you during the day, add them to your list.

The self-reward list is a fun learning experience about yourself and what matters most to you. Now that you have your ideas down, keep them in an open spot. You could also have them in an area where others can see them. One day your child or partner may bring you a chocolate-mint ice-cream cone for no reason at all, but as a display of love and an act of kindness. The list does not necessarily need to be private (unless there are personal or "adult" self-rewards listed that are not appropriate for children or others to view). Your self-rewards will help you focus on the positive steps that have moved you forward in your dance so that your energy can be directed towards positive areas of growth (as opposed to focusing on the negative "setbacks" that are inevitable on the dance floor).

Using Our Self Rewards for Success

How do we use *self-rewards?* Let's go back to our individual action plans or maps. One of our examples was a person working towards full time employment. S/he was planning on reworking their resume, exploring the Internet and delivering resumes. Therefore, the self-reward can accompany the work (i.e.-having a chocolate milk while working on the resume), or the reward can have a delay period (i.e. - a massage after delivering five resumes). It is often best to engage in self-reward the same day for best results. As adults, we often can delay gratification and still learn from the experience. For example, after accepting a full-time job, book a manicure even though it may take a few weeks to get in due to waiting lists.

Using this self-reward method helps you focus on positives, persistence and progress. Some days may include ten or eleven self-rewards, others may have less. Either way, if not for progress but simple mood maintenance and self-care, you should experience one self-reward everyday to maintain a strong foundation for your dance floor and remind yourself – you are worth it!

Because *navigating* the dance is often the most time consuming, challenging and demanding, it is also the most important DANCE component in which to practice supreme self-care. When we are pursuing a destination or a goal, S. Covey, author of the *7 Habits of Highly Effective People* suggests we are off course 90 percent of the time, just like an airplane. Winds and pressure keep airplanes off perfect flight patterns from destination A to destination B. However, with the end clearly in mind, our "D"ecision of our destination, we are able to navigate back on track and reach our destination just like an airplane. Therefore, we should expect some winds of change on this journey just as the airplane in flight.

We must then make a conscious effort to take care of our mental, emotional, physical, social and spiritual selves. Just think, what have you done this week to take care of your mental health? Your emotional health? Your physical health? Your social health? Your spiritual health? This DANCE component of *navigation* can be extremely trying so you need to be ultimately strong and extra prepared.

Setbacks

These self-rewards become extremely important on those days where inevitable setbacks occur. On a day when you make a phone call (even if you left a message because a live voice was not available), you must self-reward. If earlier that day you receive what you may perceive to be a rejection letter or indication that a company is not hiring, avoid putting your energy into this element, for the dance floor will start to cave-in like quick sand. Instead, use your self-reward system to focus on the positive which is the earlier call you made. Remember *you* have the power and the choice of where to put your energy! Will it be positive, focusing on steps forward, or negative energy, focusing on setbacks? If you find yourself moping around or disappointed, that is normal. You may even *choose* to wallow in the disappointment for a while, but remember it is your choice how long you stay there!

To be discouraged is human. When we anticipate and prepare for this time we are better able to address it. Richard Lavoie works with children, families and school communities dealing with learning difficulties. In his video, *Last One Picked, First One Picked On*, he reminds us that our goal is not simply "perfection" or the end result, but that we need to look at "progress in the right direction" and reward all attempts. If you need to call a friend to apologize for harsh words you may have said and you pick up the receiver and dial the first few numbers, reward yourself. That is right –

reward yourself! No, you did not make the call yet, but you did make progress in the right direction. As long as you do not get "stuck" repeating the same behaviour, you are still making progress and that progress should be rewarded. As a society, we often fail to recognize these needs. Ingrained beliefs often need to be challenged if they are not working anymore. Start small today and reward yourself!

A. Robbins in *Awaken the Giant Within*, also speaks of our moments of defeat and states that we must remember that "God's delays are not God's denials." When we have made a decision, acted and navigated to the best of our ability across the dance floor, we still may fall down or have our toes stepped upon. This is a reality. This is life and this temporary lack of progress is a part of the dance! Do not abandon the DANCE! I repeat. Do not abandon the DANCE!

When I first "decided" to follow my heart towards a career in a new city, there were many hurdles as I navigated towards my goal. Things did not fall into place in one month, one year, or two years. There were many times when I want-ed to sprint off the dance floor and dive into the spectator stands in retreat (actually, I did on some occasions)! However, my life mantra was not, "quit when the going gets tough." I kept dancing. I had a great job, great money, great friends, yet yearned for something more. I kept telling myself, "God's delays are not God's denials."

What delays have you experienced?

_____

_____

_____

_____

Delays may include:

- financial hardships
- funding cuts
- letters that industries or agencies are not hiring at this time
- rejection letters
- unanswered cover letters
- not getting an interview for a job
- separations
- downsizing
- deaths of family or friends
- pregnancies
- wars

The list goes on and on. Have you experienced any of these? How have you dealt with your delays? What messages have you given yourself to keep your DANCE strong?
We must plod on and navigate our way by:

- making phone calls
- arranging meetings
- building personal and professional networks
- attending family functions
- applying for jobs and so on and so on.....

One day, the skies will open and your continued belief will pay off. You may not reach perfection but it will definitely be "progress in the right direction."
Check-in on your scale of 1 to 10 from Chapter 3. Where are you now? (Circle your answer).

1....2....3....4....5....6....7....8....9....10

How did you get there? What do you need to continue doing to maintain this progress?

When you feel discouraged, remember those individuals who stayed in the dance:

- Michael Jordan did not make the Grade 9 basketball team.
- Sylvester Stallone auditioned over 500 times before landing *"Rocky"*.
- Oprah Winfrey was told she would not make it in journalism because the space between her eyes was too wide.
- *Gone with the Wind* was rejected over ten times before being published.

Beyond Setbacks

There is a *really* important piece of information that must be mentioned at this point! There is a difference between disappointment or situational depression and clinical depression. Although we all have choices, there are some very real mental health issues that do exist and that *do* need professional help and support. When discussing "depressed" feelings here with regards to setbacks, I am *not* referring to clinical depression. We all feel "depressed" or "down" sometimes. However, if this depression, loneliness or sadness exists to a point that it is affecting your daily functioning, then it is time to seek help. Call your doctor, a counselling service, a parish minister or priest. Do not deal with it alone. We all have points in our lives where we need support and professional assistance. Why go through it alone?! Do yourself, your family, your friends and your children a favour – get help! This is a critical part of the foundation of the dance floor.

If you are thinking of hurting yourself or others, call 911 or your local distress centre immediately. If you know a friend or relative who is thinking of harming themselves, tell someone. Do not go through this alone – there *is* help!

Setbacks in life are normal, pain is inevitable and feelings of isolation, depression and loneliness will come knocking at your door. The human spirit is insurmountable if only we ask for help. Hang in there!

Decisions, action plans and navigation will each present their own challenges. Triumph will not come without sweat and tears. Although these first three steps will be trying, it is in "staying focused" where the *real* work takes place. Staying focused will be our biggest hurdle. However, it may also be *our finest hour!*

What else will you need to successfully navigate across the dance floor besides self-rewards? Positive self-talk!

Positive Self-Talk

What is your life mantra? Is it encouraging, empowering, calming? Or is it defeating? We have spoken of the power of language, and we know that we will believe what we continually tell ourselves. If we say to ourselves repeatedly, "I am smart, I am smart, I am smart," we will start to believe it and act in ways that demonstrate our intelligence. If we tell ourselves, "I can't pass this course, I can't, I can't, I can't," it becomes a self-fulfilling prophecy. It is easy then, when we fail, to say, "See, I knew I couldn't pass it." Imagine living life with an "I can't" versus an "I will" attitude. Your life mantras, like your decisions, are your choice! Do not accept mantras or labels that others place on you, because people can be cruel and bitter. Do not accept their negativity into your life.

Positive self-talk is very similar to powerful life mantras. Life mantras need to be empowering and positive in the long-term. Positive self-talk is what will assist us mentally, emotionally and spiritually through the navigation phase (in the short-term). Remember, what we tell ourselves, we become. What words of wisdom can you incorporate into your vocabulary *today* to empower you and keep you focussed as you navigate your way towards your goal? Sometimes others have succeeded in the area of your goal before you. What do you think their self-talk included? Can you ask them?

As much as possible, try to utilize affirmative language regarding your actions. For example:

- I Can Do It!
- Keep Going!
- Faith is Key!
- I've been through worse, I can make it again!
- I am successful!
- Get up and Move!
- I am in Control.
- Take a few deep breaths.
- This too shall pass.
- I am coping.
- We are all doing our best.
- DANCE!

Whenever possible, avoid using negative words. For example:

- *Don't* Stop!

- You *can't* quit!
- You're *not* stuck!

Sometimes this is impossible and sometimes it will work. It is much more important to use self-talk that is inspiring to you and that means something to *you* rather than making up an opposite saying for the sake of positive power. Even though a life mantra may be "Don't stop believing," it probably would be better as, "Keep on believing," or "Do believe." It is important to consider why you put your mantra in negative terms. It must mean something to *you* that way.

How do we use positive self-talk on a daily or regular basis? The most effective way is to make sure the message is coming in through as many senses as possible: eyes, ears, mouth, nose and touch. Not only will you mentally be telling yourself (silently), *I am worth it*, you should also include these other various stimulations.

Visual - Sticky notes on mirrors, in your vehicle, in drawers, and around the house at eye level
- Screen saver on your computer
Ears - Tape your voice repeating "I am worth it" and play it when you are going to sleep
- Listen to songs in which your message is included
Nose - Associate a scent (calming lavender or invigorating eucalyptus with your life mantra)
- Put these scents throughout your house, office, or vehicle
Mouth - Arrange foods to incorporate your positive self-talk message
- spell *I am worth it* with alphabet cereal
- write *I am worth it* with ketchup on eggs

Touch - Paint or write "hope" on a stone and carry it with you (hold it during meetings, interviews)

The more avenues you use to bring the positive message in, the quicker it becomes part of your language, your reality and yourself! Don't let your old negative ways of thinking bring you down.

You may have many dances going on at once. You may be at a decision place with one dance and a navigation place with another. As you know, time will keep ticking and life will keep moving along. We have come to expect the sun to rise every morning and set every night. Successful navigation is critical to living your best life.

The Power of Life Mantras and Positive Self-Talk

An eleven-year-old young woman, Margaret, believed the footwear to her future had twelve inch blades attached to the bottoms. She wanted to skate! She decided after only a few years of figure skating lessons she wanted to try figure skating summer school. She went to her parents asking to attend figure skating summer school. They said they would think about it.

Margaret did not end up going to figure skating summer school. But many things started to develop for her at that moment, things that she could not have been aware of. There were lessons of life to make her a stronger person who was more flexible and more genuine. It seemed she was temporarily off course. She needed comfort and direction but mostly hope that life would not always be filled with such disappointment.

The music Margaret heard playing on the radio the day she was told she would not be going to figure skating summer school would become her mantra, not only for healing but for life. *Don't stop believing* has always been her favourite song and probably always will be.

Perhaps the disappointment and life lesson was not about skating but about strength and spirit. Perhaps she was not meant to skate, perhaps we were all meant to DANCE!

Mantras can be very powerful. What mantras have brought you here today? What is your current life mantra? Has it served you well or does it hold you back? Do you need a new mantra to guide your life story? What will it be?

Our life mantras can change. Some serve us well temporarily to get us through a certain period of life. Others serve us best when we are dealing with particular life issues (like grief or loss). Whatever the occasion, we need to make a conscious choice to constantly be aware of the effect our mantras have on our attitude, thoughts and behaviours. Mantras need to empower and energize us. Some songs or media images speak of drugs or alcohol to numb our emotional pain. Does this type of mantra empower? Will your dance be authentic if it is an illusion? Only you can answer such questions since no one knows you better than you do!

Navigation Reflection

Take a moment to reflect on what you can do right now to bring one decision or action plan of yours closer to reality. What can you do to move in the direction of progress?

- Is there a call you should make?
- Is there an e-mail you should check or respond to?
- Is there a person you should visit?
- Is there a letter to be written or perhaps mailed?

- Is there a letter to destroy?
- Is there a card to be sent?
- Is there a kind word to be spoken?
- Is there a "random act of kindness" that you can make without anyone knowing?
- Is there a donation to be considered?

Will these decisions and actions bring you a step forward in your dance?

BRAVO! BRAVO! It is in navigating (whether forward, backward or sideways) that you truly are moving and dancing. The best is yet to come. Once you are moving across the dance floor, it will not matter if you switch your decision or switch your dance from the foxtrot to the polka. Movement is still movement. You may decide in your action planning stage to move at a different pace or in a different direction. Once the momentum is going, it is easier to keep moving and keep dancing. You are *navigating* closer to your life's desires. Feel the movement as you DANCE and live your best life!

NOTES

Chapter 5
Compassion

If you strive to give love, all else begins to come to you.
Deepak Chopra

*I*t was a Sunday morning and I was buried alive with my five fluffy pillows. I knew by the brightness of my room that the sun was up and any other day of the week I would have been up too! But this was my day of rest – Sunday. I had even put in a number of hours yesterday (Saturday) so my restful quiet sleep in time was well deserved. Silence and calm surrounded me. BRRRING... I *don't* believe it – the phone! Who would be calling at 8:20 in the morning – my friend Annie (of course) who is up breast-feeding every other hour!

I let it ring – the machine can get it. However, the shrill sound of the phone had me awake. By 8:30 I crawled out to see if there was a message (or better yet, an invitation to supper)! Nothing – no message, no invitation just a very awake woman!

Since I was up anyway, I thought what will I "decide" to do today? I guess I could try out that new church by the university.

After a quick shower and a large double-double coffee, I arrived early to mass to secure a superb seat by the window. The service started as most services do. People were packed in like sardines but at *least* I had an aisle seat with a view.

From a distance, I caught a glimpse of the preacher. Why did he look so familiar? He looked like my previous boss when I was a student in university. I scrambled for the bulletin. There was no mention of a visiting preacher. Could this really be Joseph – the social worker whom I travelled with along with eight young offenders to Camp DARE years ago?

Dare to dream, to hope, to feel,

Dare to believe, to seek, to find,

Dare to be yourself! (and DANCE)

Finally his low, strong and calm voice began to speak. A voice from my past who empowered me to believe in myself, my skills and the power of hope and change for clients. It was Joseph. "Father Joseph!"

As he spoke, his faithful voice said, "Do not judge, and you will not be judged; do not condemn, and you will not be condemned. Forgive and you will be forgiven; give, and it will be given to you...for the measure you give will be the measure you get back" (Luke 6: 27-38). Today, Father Joseph spoke of "compassion." Originally, I was uncertain about what the "C" in the dance represented – commitment, courage, change? So I asked for some divine intervention and here it was!

The "C" in DANCE is definitely Compassion. It is not commitment. The Taliban was committed. It is not courage. It takes more than courage to DANCE. The difference lies in compassion and the ability to treat all people with dignity and respect. When you make compassion a daily part of your life, your relationships at home and work will improve, your business will flourish, profits will soar and you will truly know what an authentic life worth living is all about. The DANCE floor does not belong only to you. We share it!

Sharing the DANCE floor

It is not enough to simply enter the DANCE. The true reward comes back to us in our compassion and recognition of those dancing beside and around us. We may have goals we are striving towards or values we are trying to live up to. Compassion allows us to see part of the dance through the eyes of other dancers. Through compassion we avoid stepping on others' toes or hurling around crashing into them. Not everyone is doing the same dance. Our steps may collide if we are stepping to the tempo of the tango and they are stepping to the tempo of the waltz. Compassion affords us awareness that as we dance, what we put out onto the dance floor will return to us. If we dance recklessly only for ourselves will it truly meet our goals over time?

How will you live the spirit of compassion in your life dance? How will you consciously avoid crashing into others on the dance floor? How will your soaring spirit empower and educate those who are watching from the sidelines? When you begin practicing the power of compassion you will find the answer to these questions.

Practicing Compassion

How do we live with "compassion" in our lives? *By making a conscious effort in every relationship we are in (or those which we choose to go into) to give without any expectations of taking anything back!* We should go into relationships purely to give of ourselves, out of compassion and if we get something back – that is a bonus.

We must realize the element of compassion is related to our spiritual self-care and that without it, the enjoyment phase will most likely be empty. So what can we do to actually dance compassionately through life, starting today?

It has been suggested in the 2000 hit movie with Helen Hunt, Kevin Spacey and Haley Joel Osment – that we *Pay It Forward!* In the movie, Trevor (played by Haley Joel Osment) starts a chain reaction of national goodness for his social studies project. He was inspired to think of an idea to change the world and then put it into action. He believed that he could perform random acts of kindness for three people and instead of them paying it back to him, they could *pay it forward* to three other people. These three people would in turn pay it forward and so on. The movement was powerful and did indeed change the world.

We can *pay it forward* or contribute to life in many ways every day, every hour, every minute. Guy Chopman and Ross Campbell have wrote about the five love languages – physical touch, words of affirmation, quality time, acts of service and gifts, which basically categorize the idea of paying it forward. These five types of compassion are in essence random acts of kindness. These acts are ways to demonstrate love and compassion, whether it be in a relationship with your partner, child, colleague, breakfast waitress or bus driver.

The following is a list of 50 acts of compassion. We should be striving to *consciously* commit to at least 5 acts of compassion per day!

- Welcome a new face/person
- Offer to grab an extra coffee for someone (no charge)
- Smile
- Make eye contact with the person whom you are speaking with
- Over-tip your breakfast waitress
- Take a friend to lunch

- Give your child a hug
- Tell someone you love them
- Tell someone you appreciate them in your life
- Write a thank you note
- Write a card of encouragement
- Have a firm handshake
- Console a friend by simply touching their arm
- Leave a sticky note in your child's lunch saying "I love you"
- Place a rose in your partner's briefcase
- Send flowers to a friend at work
- When you see something on sale that you know a friend would like – buy it
- Call a friend
- Take out someone else's garbage
- Cut your elderly neighbour's lawn
- Offer to take a friend to their oncologist appointment
- Hold the door for someone
- Open the car door for another
- Hold the elevator
- Help someone who has dropped their things
- Assist a child across the street
- Buy whatever children are selling on card tables on their front lawn
- Offer to babysit for a friend
- Give a flower to someone with tears in their eyes
- Let your staff leave early
- Donate your clothing to a local charity
- Make a donation to your favourite charity
- Tell a child how special they are
- Invite a person with few family or friends to your next holiday celebration

- Take your partner on a date to their favourite spot as a teenager
- Volunteer at a soup kitchen
- Put children's artwork on display
- Let the impatient person behind you go in front of you in line
- Do the dishes
- Clean the bathroom
- Give a compliment
- Forgive someone
- Help someone be their best self
- Pay for the next person's coffee at the drive through window
- Help a friend with a project
- Make someone else's bed
- Make a cake
- Take the next cab
- Give up your sweater
- Offer to pay

Expectations

Understandably, there will be expectations that arise. For example, you need something prepared or typed by a colleague and you expect it to be done within a certain time frame. You visit your doctor and expect the best possible care and medical recommendation. Those are fair expectations for services needed. In our business or professional relationships, there are almost always expectations of give and take. However, you can always make the choice regarding expectations to make requests compassionately. It is not *what* you request that matters as much as *how* you make your request. There is a difference between tossing a request on a colleague's desk and stating impatiently, "I need this yesterday," versus attaching a friendly note with a smile, "I know you're busy, but I truly needed it yesterday." Compassion can always play a part in your communication with others.

Apart from professional or business relations, there are a variety of other relationships where you might simply give. If you do have certain expectations of someone, it can help to reframe them as preferences (they don't affect you as much if they do not come true).

For example, a parent I knew, John, "expected" his teenage daughter to thank him whenever he drove her anywhere. When his spirited teen defiantly refused, John became livid and hostile driving a wedge further and further between them. When John changed his *expectation* to a *preference*, his perception of events changed dramatically. John *preferred* that his daughter acknowledge him by saying "thanks," but if it didn't happen he no longer let it ruin his day. He decided to continue to drive his daughter with compassion. Eventually, the "thanks" returned.

A young male, Mike, expected his friend to spend the same amount of time with him as he spent with his girlfriend. He became insulted when his friend didn't call for days. Instead, when Mike changed his *expectation* to a *preference* and shared his feelings with his friend Bob, he was able to let go compassionately. Compassion means to act with love and understanding instead of judgment.

What expectations do you hold of others? Write a list of significant people in your life. Beside their name write the expectations you have of them. Now rewrite those same expectations as preferences – how does this change your relationship? How does this change your emotional state?

Your spiritual state? Your mental state? How does compassion assist you in moving away from expectations and towards preferences?

What expectations do you hold of yourself? How would your life change if you moved your personal expectations to preferences? Do not forget the most important person in your life is *you*! If you need to let go of something, then surrender. If you need to forgive someone *or* yourself, then forgive and let go. Holding on to such guilt or resentments of hate drastically weakens your ability for compassion and therefore weakens your dance! (For further reading on "letting go" see the recommended readings at the back of the book.)

When fears hold you back!

When we make decisions, and action plans and navigate our way through life with our maps respecting ourselves and respecting others, we have made a *conscious* choice to make a difference, to make a contribution - to DANCE! We can then incorporate this element of compassion into our daily action plans to ensure this element is always present.

The importance of "compassion" cannot be under-estimated. It is actually during this segment of the dance where your finest hour will shine through! When you face your fears or apprehensions and look them square in the eye and move forward with a leap of faith, you will truly feel the fulfillment of simply being alive. Our greatest love and greatest achievements require great risk and great compassion!

Mark Twain has told us, "Courage is resistance to fear, mastery of fear; not absence of fear." Fear will always exist.

- What fears have been holding you back from living a life full of compassion?

- What small step can you take today to address this fear?
- What step can you make tomorrow or later this month to continue to address this fear?
- What can you do this week to begin experiencing more compassion in your life?
- Who do you need to spend time with this week to experience true compassion or love?
- Who can you help or support in a selfless act of giving this week? This month? This year?
- What can you secretly do to make a difference in someone else's life, without needing to take credit for it?
- Where do you need to go to encourage compassion?
- What trip or vacation can you plan that will meet your self-care needs as well as contribute to others?
- What message do you need to remind yourself daily to incorporate more compassionate language in your life?
- How can you address difficult or challenging situations or people in a more compassionate way?

What about luck?

Some of you may be thinking – but what about the element of luck? Some people simply get "lucky." Good things fall right in front of their face with little or no decision making, action plans or navigating the dance floor. They simply get lucky.

A student, Harry, was told, "your co-op placement will be for eight months with Company X." No real decision or planning, yet off he went to "learn" at Company X. The company was small and just starting out. When his placement was done they kept him on. Within a few years they marketed a product that would be a huge success in the age of technology. Company stocks skyrocketed and Harry became a multi-millionaire before his 25th birthday. Some people may say "good decisions" put money in the bank. Some people may say "luck." Either way, it becomes especially important for these individuals to experience and express the element of compassion if they are to truly DANCE!

If an individual has not had to make many real decisions or navigate through difficult times, they may choose to simply move to *enjoyment!* However, we have all heard of the millionaires who are unhappy even though they have all the money in the world. You see, they are not participating in the DANCE. They are simply living in "DANE" which really equates with living in vain or in pain. Without the element of "C"ompassion, one will never truly find their authentic life worth living or worth "dancing" because compassion is a critical element in the DANCE model.

It is those individuals who may have appeared to have experienced some element of luck who will have to try extra hard to be aware of their compassionate contribution to society. They experience health concerns, financial concerns, social or family crises just as much as the next person. Compassion will be their saving grace! However, we cannot change others or the illusion of "luck" that may exist. As long as you are practicing compassion on the dance floor of life, that is where your energy needs to be. When we are dedicating our time and energy to our action plans, we are primarily using our mental functions. When we are navigating across the dance floor, we are actually physically maneouvering. Our "compassion" component deals with our spiritual selves and our sense of contribution and leaving a legacy.

A Story of Compassion

As a social worker, there are many populations and people to support on their journey in life. I feel quite confident accompanying most people, but there are a few groups that I find challenging. I knew I would not be able to work regularly with some groups, but I still made a decision to face my greatest fears and contribute in some way. That's when I heard about the camp for children and their families living with cancer. The thought of these young children facing the daily trials of living with cancer and not knowing what tomorrow would bring broke my heart. I knew I needed to support and help them in what could be their final summer. Little did I know the contribution these children and families would give to me would outweigh any contribution I could have possibly made to them.

After hearing of this camp and the wonderful things they offered, I knew I would go. I needed to seek out someone to go with, to support me! That was the summer I met my friend Dave. Although we didn't know each other well, when I shared my story of wanting to go to this camp and support these young spirits he simply replied, "Yeah, I'll go!" Although I knew little about his motives or his life, I knew he was a man of his word and a man of honour. We were going to support these families and children.

The decision was made and the action plan started. We needed to call and inquire about volunteer opportunities. We needed to look at appropriate dates of availability and so on. I made the call. We packed and were off. For three years, Dave and I committed ourselves to making the lives of those children and their families the best week at camp it could be. Before we left we would go shopping and buy footballs, candy and craft material to ensure a week full of fun and excitement. When each family arrived at camp, they were assigned a "Special Friend" who would spend the week with them. The special friends were either staff or volunteers. Every family had at least one special friend and our role was to be of support and assistance for them all week. If parents needed down time, we would be there. If kids needed to talk, we would be there. If children needed to go to the nurses station for treatment, we would be there. If staff needed to prepare for an evening program, we would be there. The family week, lasting for six days and five nights, was about giving. It was about compassion. I had tried to make a conscious life choice to add compassion to my life dance.

In the second year, my special friend was "Jake" and his family. Jake seemed fairly quiet and reserved for a seven-year-old. He was very self-conscious about losing his hair and wore his Chicago Bulls ball cap constantly. Although most of his family had arrived on Day 1, Jake and his father arrived together on Day 2 because he had a chemotherapy treatment at his local hospital. In arriving late, some of the other children had started to make friends but Jake remained close to his parents and declined my numerous attempts to get him to meet other children. On Day 4 he was off again to the hospital, his treatment was the type that he could not have administered at the on-site nurses station like most of the other children. Unlike Dave's special family who were loud and lively and wanted to try everything, my special friend needed extra time and understanding. My work was cut out for me.

After evening program where "Elvis" showed up to bring us some good old rock and roll, it was time for bed. All parents usually went over to parents' lounge to relax in the evenings and staff and volunteers took turns babysitting at different cabins. It was my night to babysit in the cabin where Jake and his family were. There were two other families in the cabin as well. Lucky for me, after a few stories and songs, lights were out and all the children in the cabin were fast asleep. My night was going to be a breeze...or so I thought.

At first it was just a few whimpers. I thought he would resettle. Then, loud tossing and turning and then all out screams loud enough to wake the country. "Please Mom, No! Please make them stop! Please Mom, Please – no more needles." I flew to the bed where the sound was coming from. Of course he was on a top bunk and in hurtling the ladder banged my head into the ceiling. It was Jake. Lots of children cry and I had seen night terrors, but I had never seen this.

After I tried unsuccessfully to console him, I bolted out the main door and asked a volunteer passing by to get Jake's parents in the parents' lounge. They had seemed so grateful and excited to have a couple hours out with other parents, to just sit back and relax. Now I was telling someone to send them back because I couldn't calm their terrified son. I felt ashamed and utterly useless.

By the time I got back to his bunk bed, his sisters were awake and I could hear them whisper to each other "Not again." His mother arrived with lightning speed. She held him and rocked him back to sleep. She smiled and told me this happens often but it had not happened in a while – not to worry! My goodness, this happens *often*?! I struggled for ten minutes with this child's fears and trauma. This was Jake's mother's life. This was Jake's father's life. This was Jake's sister's life and this was Jake's life. This family was living with cancer. For a moment, their story, their pain but most of all their courage touched my soul. Every day was a DANCE! And every day "C"ompassion made the dance bearable.

I awoke to the sly sense of humour of numerous fathers, (pretending to be construction workers) at our building known as the "staff and volunteer cabin." Another glorious day had begun! At breakfast, everything was just as usual. Jake's father arrived with a sunny smile that would light up the room. His positive attitude was just another beacon of light in a place where the similar energy and inspiration of the staff members could already reassure anyone that there *are* indeed angels among us.

I asked Jake what he wanted to do today. "I don't know" was the quiet reply. His father and mother gave him a list of options but his energy level simply seemed low. After a bit, he whispered something to his mom and she replied "We can sail if you want." For a moment, I witnessed the spark of excitement in his eyes and so it was decided - today we would sail! I would be granted the privilege to accompany this special family on a family outing and it became very apparent to me that I was not a "special friend," but rather, they were a "special family."

It did not take long to gear up with our life jackets and hop aboard the sailboat. Our staff member had knowledge and expertise on sailing etiquette and we were out in the middle of the man-made lake before we knew it. We were all enjoying the sun and peacefulness of the water as we watched other campers on shore frolicking at the beach, playing frisbee and puddle jumping.

Then it happened, the moment of truth! A moment of compassion where I would need to accept that there is more than one person on this dance floor of life. Would I dance or sit it out? These opportunities for showing compassion happen to all of us every day!

The staff member looked at Jake with anticipation and fun and asked, "Do you want to jump in Jake?" Now, at first, in my naive way I smirked, thinking, "Are you crazy? This muddy brown algae looking scum water and you are encouraging him to jump in!" Everything else we encouraged him to try this week he had declined, why would this be different? Before he could reply, she looked at me and said, "I bet your special friend Deb will go in!" What! Are you kidding? That scummy water?! Reeds and logs floating about – on the inside I replied, "Not a chance," but luckily for me, my self-care dance floor foundation was strong enough for me to remember to stop and think before I spoke. And for only the second time that week, there was a sparkle in his eye as he looked right at me and asked "Are *you* going in Deb?" To which I thought "DANCE Deb –just DANCE!" and I confidently replied, "You bet!" With that reply, I jumped overboard with a small, shy reserved and excited spirit at my heels!

Before I knew it, my decision to dance had inspired others to join us as well. Other adults in the boat, wanting to enjoy the water, jumped in. Even his father was among us. My *decision* to DANCE and *act* had a positive ripple effect on the dancers around me. It was not about me or my needs, it was about compassion and putting Jake's needs and wants and desires ahead of my own temporarily.

We swam around in the mud and algae for about twenty minutes. Jake doggy paddled with a grin ear to ear, as others around the boat encouraged and applauded him. His mother held back tears as his father hugged him. In facing his fears, he was living his best life. In facing mine, I had experienced my finest hour! We were dancing!

Often when you make a choice to help others and focus on someone else other than yourself, the effect ripples throughout the lives around you, making a difference in ways you will never even know about. It is the dance of compassion! It is unfortunate that it takes a tragedy like September 11 to truly witness how compassionate people can be and to see how they incorporate compassion into their lives?

Who do you know who does this regularly in their daily life? How do they share the dance floor? How can you incorporate the same kind of compassion in your life and start a ripple effect?

I suppose there were many lessons to learn that summer, yet some lessons were more profound than others! I believe big lessons come in small packages. Never underestimate the learning and healing power of children!

I believe there are angels among us! Every day we have the potential to witness them, if only we open up our hearts and minds. Every day we have the potential to be one if only we open up our souls. I believe one person *can* make a difference if they choose to DANCE! Making a difference will always have a ripple effect if you are strong enough to jump in and put the ripple in motion.

Your story of Compassion

Stories of compassion can be quite powerful, fueling us and others to continue to *pay it forward*. Sometimes we forget these fine hours and forget we have a compassionate side but we must *not* forget. We must let this side of ourselves flourish and grow. Your story may be short or long. Whatever your story of compassion is, write it down and read it again and again to remind yourself of the true spirit of the DANCE.

The incredible possibilities of your journey are endless – limitless. Every hour of every day you are constantly faced with opportunities to practice compassion.

- When the elderly man is struggling to get his walker through the mall door - you have a choice to DANCE.
- When the frustrated mother behind you in line is dealing with her spirited child just hoping the line will move quicker – you have a choice to DANCE.
- When a colleague drops his day-timer in the hall - you have a choice to DANCE.
- When the car beside you can't seem to get a break getting into the lane they need – you have a choice to DANCE.
- When a young student asks for your words of wisdom as they want to start a business like yours – you have a choice to DANCE.
- When you see someone looking lost and you know where you are - you have a choice to DANCE.
- When a homeless person asks for change - you have a choice to DANCE.
- When you see a car that is stuck - you have a choice to DANCE.
- When someone yells at you or ridicules you - you still have a choice to DANCE.
- When a person gathers all of their courage to ask for help – you have a choice to DANCE.

Your power of compassion is limitless. Start a ripple in the waters of life and it will ripple back to you.

Do you know when I believed beyond a shadow of a doubt that the "C" must be for compassion? It was when I returned home to check my call display feature on the telephone. My friend had not called that morning. The name displayed was not familiar at all. My silent morning slumber had been shaken by a stranger – a wrong number. Apparently, I was meant to be up and dancing. A coincidence? Maybe not. The universe was giving me a message. Be aware of these moments and *manage* your coincidences. Managing these moments will allow you to DANCE and live your best life!

NOTES

Chapter 6
Enjoy and Evaluate

If a man insisted on being serious, and never allowed himself a bit of fun and relaxation, he would go mad or unstable without even knowing it.   *Herodotus*

*H*orns honking, whistles blaring, detours, babies crying, urgent messages, colleagues yelling, phones ringing, 50 new messages, employers complaining, partners not listening, children whining, long line ups, unreturned phone calls, poor decision makers, car pools, airport hassles, language barriers, deadlines, fast talkers, road rage, careless drivers ......Welcome to life!

When did it get so complicated? When did it get so frantic? When did life get so impersonable?

As you have just spent the last several days or weeks putting your dance shoes on, approaching the dance floor and beginning the dance with all its ups and downs, it is now time to simply be still and enjoy. Even though the fast paced world we live in revolves around us, let us now make it a priority to stay focused on the end we had in mind and enjoy the dance.

The bells will still ring, the traffic will still get congested and the children will still cry. However, you did not invest all that time and energy into something you valued and believed in just to watch it unravel in the end. It is time to reap what you have sown and relax in the season of the harvest.

Many people spend hours deciding, planning, acting and navigating to quickly exhale and begin the process all over again. If we do not stop to smell the roses, we will never truly experience the joys and growth of the journey. Life will continue to pass us by where our goals may be met, money made, and productivity increased, but without making time for enjoyment, emptiness will return. This pattern of unfullfillment will repeat itself again and again until the final lesson of exhaling and enjoying is truly lived, truly experienced and truly felt. Stop and *enjoy!*

How do I truly ENJOY?

Unlock your heart and unleash your passion, for you hold the answers to your heart's enjoyment within. The key is this – *slow down.*

To experience the moment, you must give yourself permission to be still and allow yourself time to experience the moment using all your senses. Sight. Smell. Sound. Touch. Taste. Intuition.

1. Change Gears. Go to a tranquil or peaceful place (either within your home or within nature).
2. Stop Doing. Start Being. Be still and focus on your breath. Remember, life is breathing you.
3. Look around. What do you see? What do you appreciate about what you see? What are you grateful for?
4. Inhale. Smell the various aromas around you. What meaning do you attach to each? Do you need to replace these associations with something more empowering?
5. Listen. What do you hear? What is being whispered just for you? Really listen for the message. Absorb it. Do not try to force it or push it away. Just listen.

6. Taste. Feel the marvels of your mouth. What are you experiencing?

7. Feel the Energy. Close your eyes and feel what is happening *around* your body. Feel what is happening in your body. Sit with this feeling for awhile. Release your emotions and let go until the stillness returns. Open your eyes.

8. Exercise your attitude of gratitude. What are you grateful for at this moment in time?

9. Be Still. When your mind starts wandering to some other thoughts (an assignment, an argument, grocery list) just stop. Do not get upset with yourself. Just say to yourself, "oops- there I go again," and come back to the moment.

10. Breathe. Before you were just *aware* of your breath. Now you are going to bring some control to your breathing. Inhale for 3 seconds. Hold it for 3 seconds. Exhale for 3 seconds. Be empty for 3 seconds. If you can increase this exercise to 4 or 5 seconds, then do it. Life is breathing you. (We will address this breathing process in more depth in Chapter 7).

When do you make time to simply enjoy?

Today! We should include a period of stillness into our daily routines. We do not necessarily have to do all ten steps but we do need to be still. Some people form a morning ritual or evening ritual. Some people meditate. Some people have a special place or sanctuary where they go to be still. Regardless of the time of day or place, we all need to be still and enjoy a moment of peace daily.

For those people who insist they have no time, make time! Rearrange your priorities. Reschedule your day and put *you* at the top of your list. If you don't, your body will demand you take a sick day. We all know of people who were very stressed out and their body, mind and spirit eventually said, "That is enough." Do you think they were spending daily moments of enjoyment or stillness as a priority in their schedule?

You have a choice. You can either be still and relax and enjoy a few moments daily or you can let the stress build and let an internal (heart attack) or external (anger outburst) explosion happen. You decide.

What if I choose NOT to enjoy?

Prepare for pain. This book is about your DANCE. If you choose not to "E"njoy then what you have chosen to experience is the DANC. Without the "E" we have a very different word and a very different experience. Since C's and K's are often phonetically interchangeable, we could say we are also choosing to DANK.

By definition, "dank" means dreary, dark, dim, lifeless, musty and miserable. Therefore, without making a conscious choice to experience enjoyment in your dance, you are consciously choosing a lifestyle of dim, dark misery.

Do not underestimate the power of stepping back and enjoying the moment of where you are. Enjoy the DANCE and the process itself. Have you really worked this hard for a life described as dim or musty? I don't think so! Giving yourself permission to slow down, relax and connect with your experience not only helps you live life fully today, but it also helps you learn and grow from today's experiences in order to truly absorb all of tomorrow's promises.

There will also be other consequences if you choose to ignore, skip or deny yourself "enjoyment." The consequences of moving from 'danc' to 'danc' to 'danc' will include some or all of the following mental, emotional, physical, social, and spiritual consequences.

- Illness
- Ulcers
- Slower healing
- Exhaustion
- Sleep issues
- Susceptibility to disease
- Digestion issues
- Sense of disconnection from others/nature
- Loneliness
- Poor concentration
- Crying spells
- Inconsistent decision making
- Emotional moodiness
- Continued sense of urgency
- Stress related symptoms
- Headaches or migraines
- Risk of broken bones or increased injuries
- Driver/cyclist error
- Motor vehicle accidents
- Repeated layoffs
- Job loss
- Challenging relationships
- Repeated failed relationships

Sound familiar? Then start making time to enjoy your life today. When we are truly enjoying life through stillness, we can begin to look back and evaluate how far we have come and where we may want to continue to go.

It is very difficult at times to sit and be in the moment because so much needs to get done. We all feel overwhelmed sometimes and that is okay. When your mind or ego takes over to take you out of the moment, just refocus and come back to your moment. The rewards are worth it and so are you!

Evaluation Time

While I was writing this book, my friend Colette sent me an e-mail and I am so thankful that I did not delete it as I often do with extra e-mails. Many friends and colleagues send "stuff" that I do not always get a chance to truly absorb. This poem had impact, as it forced me to consider what decisions I would make for my life. The poem which follows is entitled, *"How Do You Live Your Dash?"*

I read of a man who stood to speak
At the funeral of a friend
He referred to the dates on her tombstone
From the beginning to the end.

He noted that first came her date of birth
And spoke the following date with tears,
But he said what mattered most of all
Was the dash between those years (1934 – 2003).

For that dash represents all the time
That she spent alive on earth...
And now only those who loved her
Know what that little line is worth.

For it matters not, how much we own;
The cars...the house...the cash,
What matters is how we live and love
And how we spend our dash.

So think about this long and hard...
Are there things you'd like to change?
For you never know how much time is left,
That can still be rearranged.

If we could just slow down enough
To consider what's true and real
And always try to understand
The way other people feel.

And be less quick to anger,
And show appreciation more
And love the people in our lives
Like we've never loved before.

If we treat each other with respect,
And more often wear a smile...
Remembering that this special dash
Might only last a little while.

So, when your eulogy's being read
With your life's actions to rehash...
Would you be proud of the things that they say
About how you spent your dash?

Author unknown

How are *you* spending your dash? Are you happy or content with your choices? What decisions do you need to make to enhance your life and your "dash?"

These questions are part of the process of looking back and evaluating where things are in your life dance. Look back to Chapter 2 when you first made your decisions, then Chapter 3 when you created your action plans and finally Chapter 4 and 5 when you navigated compassionately on the dance floor. We need to determine what is working and why. We also need to determine what is not working.

- What was your decision or goal to work towards?
- Were you specific and clear about your goal?
- In your action plan, where were you originally (4/10)?
- Where are you now (5/10)?
- What steps in your action plan did you take to move toward your goal?
- What steps in your action plan did you miss?
- What kept you from taking these steps?
- Do you have control of these factors?
- If so, what are you prepared to do differently now?
- If not, what do you need to change (your thinking, your attitude, acceptance)?
- Who were your supports during your navigation?
- Did they assist or deter you from meeting your goals?
- How did you act compassionately?
- Did you practice compassion daily?
- Did you try to enjoy life and be still daily?

Are Your Decisions and Plans Working?

If the answer is yes - bravo! You are dancing and living your best life. How does it feel? Enjoy, Enjoy, Enjoy! You may choose to skip Chapter 7 and move on to Chapter 8 where we will explore how to keep your current momentum going.

Following the above questions, some patterns often start to emerge. Write them down and determine what has worked well and what changes need to be made in order to DANCE. Use four columns. The first column is for what is working well. The second column is for what you want to continue to do. The third column is for what is *not* working well and the fourth for changes you need to make. An example may look like the following.

What is working well	What I need to continue to do	What is not working	Changes I need to make
-sending out resumes daily -doing follow up calls	-read classified ads daily -continue with follow up calls	-exploring job opportunities through family and friends	-explore other options for new jobs (i.e. Internet work sites)

Now you can make adjustments and continue to do what is working well, making minor changes to the things that need to be adjusted. It is not like starting all over, it's just fine tuning the DANCE. You can then practice some specific moves or changes. Now is practice time. Soon you will really fly through these practice steps. You will feel so comfortable that the DANCE will become second nature. Practice. Practice. Practice.

If you have come to a point where you believe that you have followed your action plan and that you have navigated compassionately, but are still feeling "stuck" with little or no progress (and practice has not made a difference), something else may be wrong. We will need to go back and examine some other factors. Maybe it is not the DANCE. Maybe it is the *dance floor* itself.

NOTES

Chapter 7
The Dance Floor

*"To keep a lamp burning we have
to keep putting oil in it."*
Mother Teresa

*W*hen you go out dancing, you rarely pay particular attention to the actual floor itself. You just assume it is flat and sturdy, clean and safe. It's easy to keep your balance on such a consistent surface. Would you be able to dance if the floor was continually shifting? Would you be able to dance if the floor was made out of a jello-type surface? Would you be able to dance if there were lots of five foot holes in the surface, or marbles rolling everywhere? Would you want to dance on a floor planted with landmines? All of these situations would effect the safety and success of a great dance and a great life. Therefore, we need to take a moment to look at how secure *our* DANCE floor is to lead to our best dance possible.

When things are not working with your DANCE, the answer will usually be - the DANCE floor. If you are struggling with your DANCE, there may be a crack or an imbalance in the foundation of the floor. As with life, you will surely run into potholes or slippery sections where you will be bound to lose your balance. *Balance* builds the foundation of your life DANCE. Your DANCE foundation needs to be solid, smooth and sturdy.

As we know, the DANCE begins with your "decision" component. During this time, you may be sitting off in the bleachers or on the sidelines and listening to your inner wisdom of where you want your life to go (See Figure 7.1). Then, "action plans" prepare you for your life dance. Here you will be standing up, putting your dancing shoes on and tying them securely in order to start moving. "Navigation" is when you enter the dance floor and start to move to the beat of the music. "Compassion" is constant as you move across the dance floor being aware of where you are and who is around you. "Enjoying" takes place within this movement along with some time for evaluating your progress.

The components that help maintain the strength of the dance floor include;

> **M**=Mental
> **E**=Emotional
> **P**=Physical
> **S**=Social and
> **Sp**=Spiritual.

Notice the extra emotional components in Figure 7.1 that need to be nurtured in order to ensure proper maintenence of the dance floor and living your best life.

The following ideas are critical to the success of your life dance. Whenever you are struggling, come back to these elements that are the foundation of the dance floor and a major guiding principle of the success of your DANCE!

Figure 7.1

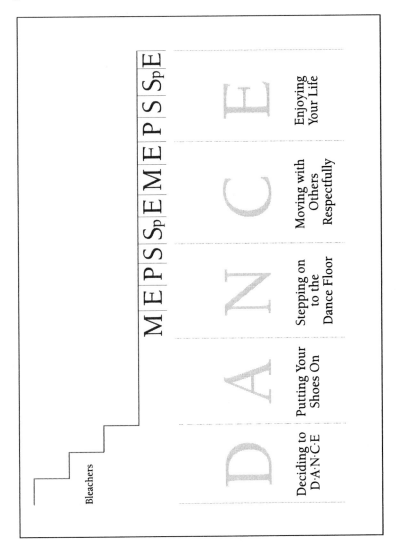

Practicing Supreme Self-Care

You will only be able to take care of your dreams, your family, your friends, your relationships, your career and your "DANCE" if you give yourself permission to take care of *yourself*. You must make private time for you or else the dance simply becomes a meaningless race. How many people do you know that have experienced health problems due to stress related illnesses? A cold may often be your body's way of saying, "You had a choice to slow down or speed up and now I make the choice for you – slow down!" Our body needs rest. Even when work demands are increasing and family members need you, it is still *imperative* to take time out for you. Personal boundaries are extremely important! We may have to say "No" or "Later" to someone who expects a "Yes" immediately.

The foundation of the DANCE floor is supreme self-care and it includes these five main components: 1) **M**ental Health 2) **E**motional Health, 3) **P**hysical Health, 4) **S**ocial Health and 5) **S**piritual Health (Or MEPSS pronounced "maps").These are the DANCE floor maps. These components will effect the shape of your dance floor tremendously. If the components are healthy and balanced, the dance floor will be sturdy and you will dance safely. If they are ignored or non-existent, the dance floor will be rocky, and your dance may not have a chance to get started.

It is unrealistic to expect perfect balance. Self-care is not about perfection, but progress in the right direction. As long as you are attempting to take care of all aspects of yourself, the goal of living your best life using the DANCE model is greatly improved. Let's start with a self-care test to see how well you are doing!

Self Care Test
<u>Mental Health</u>

- Do you read regularly?
- Are you aware of negative thoughts that creep into your mind?
- Do you address these thoughts (or let them grow)? If so, how?
- Do you exercise your mind daily?
- Do you feel in control of your destiny most of the time?
- Do you take mini-vacations (imagining yourself in your safe sanctuary)?
- Do you learn a new skill every year?
- Do you write in a journal or planner?
- Do you make time daily to "be still?"

<u>Emotional Health</u>

- Do you set aside at least ten minutes a day to do something you truly love?
- Do you set aside a time each day to be with (or connect with) someone you love?
- Do you have a personal life mantra that empowers you?
- Do you affirm yourself daily?
- Do you have a word to automatically bring about a positive response in your body? Do you use it regularly?
- Do you use the words "please" and "thank you" regularly?
- Do you exercise your compassionate heart daily (performing random acts of kindness)?
- Do you have two or three activities that you can easily do to relax readily available to you?

- Do you listen to music or sounds to relax?
- Do you feel in control of your emotions most of the time (or are your emotions controlling you)?
- Do you acknowledge people regularly as you meet them on the street?
- Do you drive respectfully and allow others in front of you?
- Do you reward yourself for your efforts rather than final accomplishments?
- Do you express your feelings openly (verbally, written words, or creative arts)?
- Do you seek out professional help when dealing with larger issues?

<u>Physical Health</u>

- Do you exercise your body regularly?
- Do you visit your doctor for regular check-ups?
- Do you visit your dentist regularly?
- Do you take your practitioner's advice when they refer you to specialists?
- Do you follow doctor's prescriptions?
- Do you maintain a healthy weight?
- Do you eat healthy foods (like fruits and vegetables) daily?
- Do you drink 6-8 glasses of water each day?
- Are you aware of where tension resides in your body?
- Do you partake in preventative health practices (massage, vitamins, etc.)?
- Do you avoid illegal drugs or substances?
- Do you get six to eight hours of sleep regularly?
- Do you use breathing techniques to deal with stress?

Social Health

- Do you spend quality time with family regularly?
- Do you make time to be with close friends weekly?
- Do you feel close to those around you?
- Do you connect with a social group at least once a month?
- Do you have a regular "date" night with your partner?
- Do you meet with people at work occasionally outside of the structured work day?
- Do you invite conversation when in social environments (gym, grocery store, mall)?
- Do you enjoy your own company?
- Do you trust most people?
- Do you ask for help when you need it?
- Do you make time for important people in your life?

Spiritual Health

- Do you commune with nature and appreciate the beauty in your life?
- Do you exercise your faith daily?
- Do you use your five senses when relaxing?
- Do you have a plan to leave a legacy?
- Do you have positive or peaceful images throughout your home or work space?
- Do you listen to spiritual music?
- Do your read spiritual or inspirational literature?
- Do you share your faith with others?
- Do you meditate, pray or practice yoga?
- Do you know and live your top 5 values?
- Do you know your life purpose?

If you answered "NO" to 3 or more questions in each category, your DANCE floor is wavering. Take action to make it more solid and sturdy in that area of your MEPSS. This self-care process will help you DANCE. The time and energy of this investment into your personal self will be well worth it in the end.

Figure 7.2

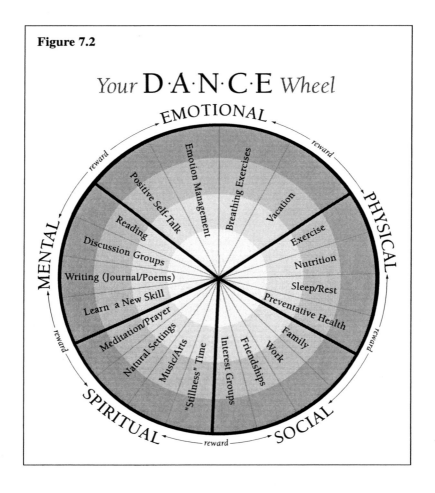

Your D·A·N·C·E *Wheel*

Your DANCE Wheel (Figure 7.2)

The 5 sections of the DANCE wheel (Figure 7.2) represent balance with your mental, emotional, physical, social and spiritual health. Take a look at these five main areas. Now rank your level of satisfaction in each individual section within the 5 main areas out of 4 (1 being not satisfied = inner circle and 4 being very satisfied =outer circle). Shade in these areas. Once again, notice the size of the emotional component compared to the others and also the fact that self-rewards surround the wheel as a reminder of their significance. The new perimeter represents your level of balance in the dance of life. If this were a tire on a car, how smooth would your ride in life be?

Let's take a deeper look at the 5 components of the DANCE floor.

1. Mental Health

One way to improve your mental health is to build your knowledge. Knowledge changes you. Knowledge can fuel the dance.

R. Sharma (1997: p.117) writes, "Read regularly. Reading for thirty minutes a day will do wonders for you. But I must caution you. Do not read just anything. You must be very selective about what you put into the lush garden of your mind. It must be immensely nourishing. Make it something that will improve both you and the quality of your life." Furthermore, he suggests that all problems you will ever face have already been experienced by someone else. Therefore, the answers and solutions are out there. You just need to find them. Read the right books and learn how others have handled their challenges. You don't have to reinvent the wheel. Utilize other's strategies for success and watch for the improvements you witness in your own life.

Whatever decision you choose to embark on in your life DANCE, there is a real possibility that someone has already been there and you can learn from their DANCE! Therefore, we should READ! READ! READ! If you can afford an hour a day, go for it! If you can only spare ten minutes, start there…but read! Remember, "knowledge can be power," but as R. Sharma (1997: p.115) points out, "knowledge is only potential power. For the power to be manifested, it must be applied." It is one thing to decide on a goal, but then you need action plans before the navigation process can bring your dreams to life.

In his "Ten Day Mental Challenge" in *Awaken the Giant Within*, Anthony Robbins (1991, p.309) talks about our patterns of thinking. He states, "A new level of thinking is now required in order to experience a new level of personal and professional success…our old patterns of allowing our minds to be enslaved by the problems of the moment must be broken once and for all." He believes our old patterns have brought us to where we are, but they will not get us to where we want to go. Therefore, he introduces us to a mental diet where it becomes obvious just how powerful our thoughts can be. His mental diet encourages people to avoid any "unresourceful" thoughts or emotions for 10 consecutive days. Instead of putting your mental energy into any negative thoughts, put your energy into a solution. Ten days is a challenge, but try it! People are what they believe (or what they say to themselves daily or hourly). Our language is very powerful. Use it to your advantage.

If we continue to tell ourselves "I am broke, I am broke, I have no money," our mind, a powerful force, hears this message and not only believes it, but subconsciously makes decisions that reinforce this statement leading to what has ultimately been known as the "self-fulfilling prophecy."

A person who tells themselves they are broke may invest in an unstable stock, rationalize why they need the most expensive pair of sunglasses, lend five dollars to a friend they know will not pay it back and then repeat to themselves, "See, I told you I was broke."

Another individual may say to themselves, "I am rich, I am rich, I am rich!" They will walk and talk confidently as though they are financially secure. They will attract more good fortune to themselves. In fact, this person may actually have less money than the person who was going around saying to himself "I am broke," but their attitude is positive and focuses on abundance which affects their mental health in a powerful way!

What do you continually tell yourself about your life? Is this language empowering you and your life? Can you rephrase your statement using even more powerful language? As Anthony Robbins suggests, we must take charge of our mental life metaphors. We must take charge of our mental health.

As part of our mental health self-care, we need to expand and challenge our most powerful tool - our mind. This knowledge definitely contributes to the foundation of the DANCE floor and will help us navigate smoothly towards a life worth living. As Marcus Aurelius Antonius, the Roman emperor, once told us, "Our life is what our thoughts make it."

What can you do today to enhance your mental health?

_____

_____

_____

_____

2. Emotional Health

Emotional health is the area of the DANCE floor that usually creates the most difficulty for people. Emotions are very powerful and they may keep you from dancing a successful dance. So who is in control? You *or* your emotions? Generally speaking, if you do *not* hurt yourself or others (verbally or physically), or damage property, you are usually in control. However, if you do hurt yourself, others, and/or damage property your emotions are in control, leaving your DANCE floor unstable.

Getting Emotions Out

There are basically three main outlets for our emotions: mouth, hands, and feet. Most of us naturally gravitate towards one outlet or another. Regardless of the outlet, as long as you are not hurting yourself (punching walls), others (swearing at people) or damaging property (breaking personal items), you can successfully deal with your emotions. Dealing with these emotions strengthens your DANCE floor. Here is a chart demonstrating various ways to use these outlets to express your emotions and strengthen your emotional health.

	POSITIVE CHOICES	**NEGATIVE CHOICES**
MOUTH	-breathing -"I" messages (I feel..., when you..., I want...) -talking to a trusted friend	-swearing -gossip/rumors -spitting -biting -yelling
HANDS	-drawing -journal writing -computer games -stress ball -cooking -playing catch	-punching someone -rude written letters -sending inappropriate email -breaking or damaging someone's property
FEET	-soccer -jogging -rollerblading -swimming	-kicking a pet -kicking a wall

Breathing Exercise

Deep breathing has been proven to be one of the most effective ways to deal with difficult and strong emotions. Bringing fresh air into our lungs and physical system can help us deal more effectively with any situation we are in. We need to inhale the oxygen (fresh air) into our lungs which travels through the bloodstream to our brain and allows us to process information and potentially make healthy decisions. We need to get oxygen to our muscle groups to relieve tension and help us relax. We need to release the carbon dioxide through exhaling to remove excess poison from our system.

If we take shallow breaths, we are not getting enough oxygen to our brain and muscles in order to deal with challenging situations. We will remain tense and are in a position to make poor decisions.

Therefore, deep breathing is critical to our emotion management. We need to learn these strategies for our own day to day coping. We also need to teach these skills to our children to help them deal with their many emotions.

The Breathing Process (using a minimum 3 second count)

1. Inhale (over a count of 3 seconds).
2. Hold (for a count of 3 seconds). This is the most important step which is the major difference between shallow and deep breathing. Oxygen is being transferred into the lungs and carbon dioxide is being transferred out. Be sure to include this step!
3. Exhale (for a count of 3 seconds).
4. Empty (remain empty for a count of 3 seconds).

Practice this 4 step process either by counting aloud, internally, or by counting on your fingers until it becomes second nature.

When you are comfortable doing a 3 second count, increase your count to 4 or 5 seconds for each step. Individuals who practice extreme meditation or yoga often hold their counts for up to 10 seconds. As long as individuals are counting for 3 seconds for each step, a significant positive change will affect their entire physiological system.

Repeat the process often and practice whenever possible (the grocery line, driving, watching TV). Feel free to use it during important meetings or if you are having difficulty falling asleep. Focus on your breath and not the problems or worries of the day. Remember, life is breathing you.

When you practice using this breathing technique, there is a better chance of you being in control instead of your many emotions. Breathe, Breathe, Breathe.

Letting Go

When our fears, our anger, our disappointment, our hurt, our jealously, our rage, our frustrations, or our resentments dominate our day, it seems safe to say that our emotions are in control of our life. Our emotions and their power, however, can be a huge positive channel for change if we channel those feelings in the right direction (they can also be dead weights cementing our footwear to the floor and keeping us from dancing). If we truly want to dance through this lifetime, we will need to let go of those over-powering negative emotions that keep us from experiencing true joy.

It has been said there are only two true emotions: joy and fear. It is all of those *fear* emotions (anger, jealousy, resentment, etc.), that we need to try and deal with or let go of. If we choose to keep them, how will it affect our DANCE?

Let's go back to the beginning. Your *birth* day! The day the world welcomed you into the universe with "It's a girl/boy!" Your story began at that time and your life unfolded. The chapters of your book have brought you here to this spot today (regardless of your age). Many lessons have unfolded and you need to acknowledge and learn from them. If not, your powerful emotions will keep you stuck in the past adding significant weight to the soles of your footwear. It is very difficult to dance with those heavy weights!

What can you do today to let go of a hurt from the past? Is it time to forgive? Who? Yourself? Another? What needs to happen in order for you to move toward forgiveness, to move toward closure, to move toward inner peace?

Keep in mind that as soon as you choose to let one hurt or fear go, another hurt will awaken within you. The process of letting go and not hanging on to past issues is a lifelong process. Also, remember the power of these emotions have the potential to be *transformed* into amazing energies. I have watched a mother who had lost a child become one of the most inspirational pediatric nurses you could ever imagine. I have watched a colleague diagnosed with cancer redirect her energies into one of the most successful careers imaginable. I have seen a soccer player taken out of the game in his prime get back up and become a motivational coach - inspiring young children and youth to be the best people they can be. I have witnessed a young man living with cancer initiate the "Marathon of Hope" to raise awareness of cancer research throughout the country. Although Terry Fox is no longer with us, his legacy lives on every September when cities across our country continue to organize his Marathon of Hope.

If anyone had reason to sit the dance out with the shackles of resentment, pain, grief and hurt, these people did. However, in letting go of the negative and instead putting their energy of those fears into something more, they have made a difference! They have left a legacy! They have chosen to dance!

Who do you know that has chosen to let go? How do you know they made that decision? What unique characteristics or character traits do they possess? Which of those same characteristics do you share? What resentments or pain did they need to get past? With your best guess, how do you think they humanly managed it? What strategy can you borrow or share? What can you learn from their process or life story?

If someone you know or trust and respect has gone through this process of letting go and choosing to dance, ask them for their success story! What did they need to tell themselves? What actions did they need to take? Did they need to seek professional help? If so, who would they recommend? Is it not worth asking the questions in order to let go and move on? Although the "letting go" process can be challenging, there are many great works in local bookstores on this process of healing and forgiveness. Find one that fits for you. If you do not find a book that is helpful, call your local counselling agency to get support. They are there for you!

A Story of Channeling Emotions

I was a "Big Sister" for almost five years and our favourite activity when we got together was to go to the movies. One day my "little sister" Josie begged me to see a particular movie. She had heard about it at school and from friends. I *totally* did not want to see it.

Josie (then fourteen) and I entered the theatre to watch *Apollo 13*. The only reason I really agreed to see this extra long film was because I liked Tom Hanks. After the film, I had a new appreciation for Ed Harris as well. This movie has become one of my top 5 hits of all time.

There was a moment in the movie, when the crews on earth had worked feverishly to re-create what was going on in the spacecraft in order to get the three astronauts home safely. An enormous team of professionals on earth had come together with all their skill sets and now they had to wait. They had put their energy of fear and anxiety (negative) into a proposed solution (positive) for the problems being faced in space. They had done all they could do. The mission was now out of their control and the whole world watched. One of the lead men on earth asked questions which focused on the reality that the ship had three minutes to re-enter the earth's atmosphere. If the re-entry took longer than three minutes, they would simply assume the men were not coming home.

If they had let their emotions be in control (fear, anger, and anxiety), they never would have been able to creatively re-create the situation and assist those men to return to earth. Instead, they took the energy from those emotions (fear and anxiety) and redirected it to re-create the situation and find a solution which lead to their finest hour.

They chose to focus on potential positive outcomes. The crew had done all they could and had "let go." Putting the energy of their fears to work, their efforts guided the Apollo 13 home. They chose to dance!

For all of those people you know who have chosen to dance, what was their finest hour? How can you bring your passion and committed energy into helping you let go of the past and refocus on the energy of your dance?

Let go of the fear. Focus your energy on joy. Take a leap of faith! Your wings will be there. If you take a leap of faith and fall, have you actually failed? What can you do today to make an investment into you emotional heath?

_____

_____

_____

_____

3. Physical Health

Most people are aware of the importance of taking care of their physical body yet many people continue to struggle with this issue. We need a solid foundation of health, not only to get us to DANCE, but to be able to truly enjoy the experience along the way.

R. Sharma speaks to the power of physical care. He addresses the need to invest at least five hours a week in some form of physical activity whether it is yoga, walking or another sport. It does not matter what physical activity we engage in. What matters is that we have set aside time for our physical selves. Sharma (1997: p.110) states:

"The ritual of physicality is based on the principle that says as you care for the body so you care for the mind. As you prepare your body, so you prepare the mind (to dance). As you train your body, so you train your mind. Take some time every single day to nourish the temple of your body through rigorous exercise. Get your blood circulating."

Do not be fooled into thinking that the only way to experience optimal health is by joining a gym. Although for some people this plan may be necessary or ideal, it is not imperative. We can still exercise and get our blood moving daily. If we want to address specific issues such as fat burning or the difference between aerobic and anaerobic activity, it will be necessary to enlist a professional's knowledge and expertise. That step is not necessary for everyone though, so do not jump ship all together. Again, it is not about "perfect fitness" but progress in the direction of taking care of your physical health. Start small, with a short walk or a few sit-ups. Remember, you know your body best and you should not start a new exercise regime without first consulting your doctor.

Perhaps individual sports like running or a gym membership are not for you. Many people enjoy the physical and social benefits of organized team sports like soccer, baseball or volleyball. Most local newspapers or community centres advertise when they are looking for new players so keep your eyes and mind open (physical health is not limited to expensive equipment or busy Nordic Tracks). Friends or colleagues often know when teams are looking for new players so let other people know when you are interested in joining a specific team. Make clear your expectations - is it for fun and recreation or various levels of competition? Either way, make the choice to take care of your physical health and secure your foundation for a successful dance through life.

Plan for Success. Be Realistic.

Now as much as we may like a full day out on the golf course or at the spa, these optimal situations are not always possible. So start small. A ten minute walk, a fifteen minute bath or a visit to the driving range are realistic goals. Do not surrender to that voice in your head that claims "You don't have time." Make time! You are your greatest asset. How valuable will you be to your children, your team, your employer or employees if you are continually miserable or sick?

I often hear from various parents who I work with, "I can't! I can't find the time because..." and the list begins. R. Sharma (1997, p.121) states, "The real problem is that too many people suffer from that dreadful disease known as excusitus." We all make excuses but sometimes we need to acknowledge and accept the choices we have made in our lives. We "can't" make time or we "choose" not to make the time. Value yourself. Ask for *your* needs to be met. Be good to yourself or nobody else will! If you want to DANCE, you need to give yourself permission to care for your physical health.

A number of these same parents later came back and said they *did* make a *small* amount of time for themselves by taking a walk or going for a bike ride. They later admitted, "If I hadn't have made the time, I would have had a nervous breakdown." Before making the effort to take care of themselves, a chained force seemed to be leading or dragging them around the dance floor. Then, in setting some personal boundaries and giving themselves permission to take care of themselves, they regained control of their dance.

What can you do today to take care of your physical self?

_____

_____

_____

_____

4. Social Health

Your social health relates to your relationships with family, friends, neighbours, colleagues, employers and everyone you come in contact with during the course of your day. In order to keep the DANCE floor stable, you must make an investment in your relationships. We are all social beings. Even introverts (who prefer being alone) still need contact with others regularly. Some of us need more social contact than others.

S. Covey, in the *7 Habits of Highly Effective Families*, encourages us to make "deposits" as opposed to "withdrawals" into our relationship bank accounts. We need to build our relationships by spending quality time together, communicating openly, and doing things for each other. This suggestion may mean that the dishes and laundry will pile up. That can be okay. In order to build and maintain your social health, you need to ensure you are spending time with the most important people in your life.

In today's society, we have e-mail, voicemail and elaborate computer systems that have affected our social connections in both positive and less than positive ways. Our family and friends may move away and e-mail becomes an important and cost effective way to communicate. However, it is less personal and your tone can be easily misinterpreted. Therefore, connection with our social circle needs to include face-to-face contact. To truly maintain social health, we need that human connection, whether it is at social events or over lunch. If the majority of your connections are electronic in nature, you may need to ask yourself what you are trying to avoid? How can you get more connected? Do you need to reach out to a new social circle?

True happiness consists not in the multitude of friends,
but in the worth and choice.
Ben Jonson (1572-1637)

What can you do today to make an investment into your social health?

_____

_____

_____

_____

5. Spiritual Health

When it comes to our spiritual health a lot of confusion and apprehension exists. Most people admit that when they hear this word "spiritual," they associate it with organized religion. Over the past few decades, we seem to have moved away from the traditional definitions of religion and have moved toward a philosophy of openness and acceptance. For the purpose of the foundation of your DANCE and supreme self-care, what we really mean by "spirituality" is the idea of listening to yourself and being in touch with your higher power - whatever that may be. It is a definition that comes from you (and perhaps your culture) and therefore "fits" for you. Spiritual health is very personal and private reflecting your own values. Even in most religions, people will admit that not all of the ideas, traditions or rituals "fit" for them. Some people accept the positive and negative doctrines of their church. For other people, rather than accepting and integrating the pieces that "fit" for them and leave the rest, they choose to leave their church, synagogue, mosque or place of worship and then in fact lose the positives that they experienced as well.

Maintaining your DANCE floor will require that you acknowledge your spiritual self and look at ways to strengthen it. Wayne Dyer, in *Your Sacred Self*, reminds us that we are not human beings having a spiritual experience. We are spiritual beings having a human experience. Regardless of your beliefs around these thoughts, to deny this spiritual aspect of yourself will create inconsistencies on your DANCE floor. Inconsistencies simply make it more challenging to dance.

In the past, I took a course at the University of Western Ontario on self-healing. Our professor described the concept of different religious bases with this analogy. He stated that if you are driving to Toronto from London (or Seattle from Chicago) it does not truly matter if you drive a blue minivan, black sports car or red transport truck. It does not matter how you get there. It is the *destination* that counts. What he was suggesting was that it is less important whether you are Moslem, Catholic, Protestant, or Hindu, than if you are in touch with your belief system at all. What matters is that you are aware of and in touch with your higher power.

Spiritual health will help give you a sense of purpose and meaning in your life. It will help guide your DANCE process in a direction that truly fits your belief system. You may be physically, mentally and emotionally fit, but without a sense of purpose guiding you from the depth of your being (your soul), most accomplishments will continue to leave you with a feeling of emptiness. That part of you (your spiritual self) will still be slumbering or sleeping and your DANCE floor will not be as stable or strong as it could be. For most people, there exists a sacred or safe place they can go (perhaps a setting in nature) where they are able to be still and connect with their higher power within. Some people meditate there. Some people pray. Some people simply close their eyes and go within themselves to connect spiritually. We all have different practices and there are no right or wrong answers. What can you do today to strengthen your spiritual health?

_____

_____

_____

_____

Your DANCE Floor (Figure 7.3)

Imagine being a light fixture looking down upon your dance floor. These are all the components that maintain its strength and stability. (Notice the extra emotional pieces)! Create a similar floor map and indicate what you are doing for each section to maintain the health of your dance floor.

Your DANCE floor will never be perfectly maintained. Life will continue to throw the odd marble on the surface, which you will have to dodge. However, the idea of maintaining the DANCE floor goes back to one of our guiding principles which is, the better you maintain your DANCE floor (by practicing supreme self-care), the better your chances for positive decision making. The better choices you make, the better chance of living your best life!

Maintaining is not about perfection, it's about keeping everything in balance. When you put energy into taking care of your DANCE floor, you will inevitably start to notice positive changes gaining momentum around you. Then, all you have to do is to keep that momentum going!

Figure 7.3

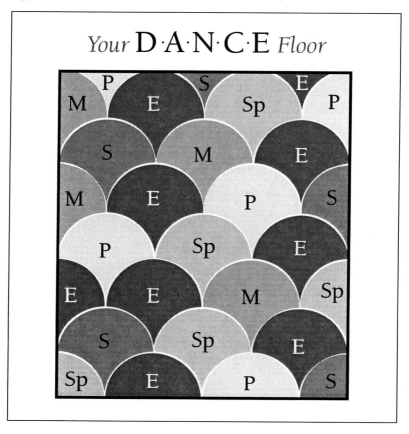

NOTES

Chapter 8
How Do I Keep the Momentum?

On with the dance! Let joy be unconfined.
Lord Byron

*I*t's working! It's working! You must be doing something right. You have made decisions that are becoming reality before your very eyes. You have set goals that you can see being achieved. You have mapped out your action plans and can witness progress on the map before you. You have been compassionate with others on the dance floor in your life and have reaped the benefits of more positive, powerful and healthy relationships. You have looked back to view where you have come from and where you are today with a sigh of contentment, peace and achievement. You are dancing! You feel great!

Now you want to know the secret of keeping this feeling of contentment and peace as part of who you are. Do you need to make more decisions about the future? Not necessarily. Do you need to revamp your action plans? Not yet. Do you need to navigate in a new direction? Maybe, but maybe not. Although these steps got you to where you are today and where you want to stay, these are not the secrets to maintaining the momentum or the secrets of enduring happiness.

The secret is to maintain the balance, integrity and stamina of your dance floor! Keep sweeping. Keep polishing. Keep scrubbing and your DANCE will keep gliding; your dance floor shining!

Secret Number One

We cannot underestimate this component of supreme self-care. When you start slacking off with your commitment to your mental, emotional, physical, social and spiritual health, you will start slipping. If you feel yourself starting to slip, that is okay. Just listen to your inner voice warning you to check in to what area within yourself needs attention.

Continue to give yourself permission to take care of you! As adults, we cannot put the responsibility of taking care of ourselves on others. It is different when we are children. We need others to care for our needs, especially our most obvious physical needs. As adults, we need to maintain this ownership of self-care. If others choose to help us or support us along the way, that is just a bonus. If our partner suggests they watch the kids so you can go to the gym- great! If they do not make the suggestion, we need to ask for our needs to be met and put this within our daily schedule. We cannot make the assumption or place that expectation on others to plan our self-care for us. We alone are responsible for our supreme self-care plan.

Continue to ask yourself:

What have I done to make an investment into my mental self today? This week?

• Have I picked up a book and read?

• Have I attended the class I signed up for regularly?

I have:

_____

_____

(Write your answer here)

What have I done to take care of my emotional needs today?
This week?
• Have I spoke with a trusted friend about what is on my mind?
• Have I released my feelings through journal writing or painting?
• Did I allow myself the time to cry when I felt the need?
I have:

_____

_____

(Write your answer here)

What have I done to take care of my physical body today?
This week?
• Have I gone on a brisk walk?
• Have I worked out at the gym?
• Have I booked that massage?
• Does cutting the grass (with the push lawnmower) count for my cardiovascular workout?
I have:

_____

_____

(Write your answer here)

What have I done to address my social self today? This week?
• Have I golfed with my social circle?
• Did I introduce myself to someone new?
• Did I open myself up to a new social group to meet new people?
(Remember, you will be the exact same person a year from now as you are today except for the people you meet and the books you read).
I have:

_____

_____

(Write your answer here)

What have I done to address my spiritual needs today? This week?
• Have I meditated? Prayed?
• Did I make an effort to be with nature (in the garden or on a nature hike)?
• Did I make time to "be still" and listen to my inner voice?
I have:

_____

_____

(Write your answer here)

Secret Number Two

In *The Wisdom of Oma,* (2003, p.44) Karen Vos Braun shares with us her Oma's 13th gift: give thanks for all the blessings in your life. "In every life, in every day, and in every moment, there is always something to be grateful for." In order to maintain this momentum you are feeling, remember to give thanks and count your blessings. We are often surprised when we take the time to notice just how many gifts are actually around us.

Oprah also encourages people to keep a daily gratitude journal. With this journal, we are to write down (not just think about, but actually commit to paper) 5 things we are grateful for. If you want to write more, feel free. You gain perspective on your problems pretty quickly. When people say they are too busy to write 5 things down they are already in a place where the momentum will be slipping. Stop and be still.

This simple practice of gratitude, along with supreme self-care, helps to keep momentum going by constantly reminding us of what we have to lose. Take a moment to remind yourself of all you have in your life right now to be thankful for (which is what you could potentially lose with poor choices). Are these assets not worth keeping? Are your decisions not worth truly examining in order to keep this momentum and feeling of inner peace and contentment?

Five things you are grateful for at this moment are:

* _____

* _____

* _____

* _____

* _____

Be still and be grateful.

A Story of Momentum

It was still that night. We were crossing the East Timor Sea. There were three main sections to the barge: cargo, first class and VIP. When a number of my backpacking group boarded with our life belongings, we had to literally step over hundreds of women and children crowded between trucks and bags of rice on the cargo level of this old ship. Babies were screaming; children rolled dice to keep busy and eyes stared at those of us coming on board who were quickly moving towards first class. Although the boat had huge windows and some of the children dangled out of these large openings for excitement, the smell was excruciating. We all looked at each other in a way that communicated, "Thank goodness we're in first class!" We joked that the ship was overloaded and it surely would not be able to float!

When we got to the first class section, it was packed with people and huge backpacks. There was no room to sit. When we finally managed to maneuver through the masses we found a corner area to sit but had to keep our backpacks on our knees because there was no room to put them. We joked again about how happy we were to have paid the extra few dollars to get into first class.

We knew the ride was approximately ten hours and we were sailing through the night. We were looking forward to some solid sleep but knew it would be challenging in our tight quarters. One of our group members had made it to the washroom and overheard that another small section (with twenty passengers) would be opening up soon for "a small price." Because we all wanted to sleep and relax in comfort, we all dug deep into our pockets for the Indonesian rupee and jumped at the man who opened the VIP section. An hour into the ride in first class, people were vomiting. Body odour was profuse. We had just been afforded some VIP space! The sweet price of personal space! A few of us played cards for a bit, a regular back-packer past time, but eventually we all spread out on the long benches for some quality sleep. We had no idea what the night would bring.

As I woke up to the bright full moon beaming in a pure black sky I realized I was freezing. I was soaked. At first I attributed my lack of balance to having just woke up, but then I heard people being sick behind me and I looked at a young man I'd been traveling with. Alex was staring out at the night with horror in his eyes and clenched the bench tightly. I stared at him in confusion and he noticed I was awake; our eyes met. He looked at me and smiled saying, "We'll be okay," but the apprehension in his tone gave him away. SPLASH! The water was bursting through the VIP windows. It felt like the windows may shatter. The water was cold and all I could think about was the Titanic. Where were our life jackets? Looking around quickly, I realized -what life jackets? There were no life jackets! Most people in our VIP room were awake and silent. The boat was rocking back and forth – side to side and front to back. We later heard the tides of the two oceans meeting in Indonesia can be quite intense, especially during the full moon!

For the next hour we all panicked in the night. Apart from the odd gagging, all you could hear was the crashing of waves against the old boat. And then it dawned on me, if I was soaking in the VIP section at the top of the boat enclosed in windows, how would those other people ever survive in the cargo section? I then lost track of where the moisture was coming from – the waves or my tears! After a few hours of human silence and fear, Alex started to talk. At first it was just the two of us, then the conversation grew. Everyone seemed to recognize the reality of the situation and knowing it was now out of our hands and up to a greater power we started to reflect on our lives. The joys. The pains. The lessons.

Hours went by and our conversation continued. We temporarily forgot about the storm and bonded through our life stories. As the dawn approached and we all disembarked safely, many things became clearer. Some days, I wish it had not taken such an intense experience to truly appreciate the gift of life. Most days I am simply grateful to be alive, happy and healthy. I will never forget what could have been our final hour, our final thoughts, our final words to each other. There is always so much to lose. Live each day to the fullest, in kindness, happiness and peace. Never miss a chance to say "I love you" or "I'm sorry." Life is precious.

You keep the momentum of your DANCE by practicing supreme self-care, gratitude and remembering what it is you have to lose. You need to remember how precious life is and that your choices today affect your chances for tomorrow. Most people will admit that what they want in life is happiness which they usually describe as some sort of calm or inner peace. How do we get there? We DANCE.

If this feeling of inner peace and calm is what you strive for, you now have the answer. The secret to the five steps to living your best life is the DANCE. You keep momentum by taking good care of yourself, being grateful for what you have and thoughtful of what you have to lose or gain. The momentum is there. You have it now within your grasp. Keep Dancing!

NOTES

Chapter 9
Celebration

We shall not cease from exploration
And the end of all our exploring
Will be to arrive where we started
And know the place for the first time.
T.S. Eliot

Although it may appear the journey is ending, your journey is really only beginning. Perhaps you thought you would join the dance of life and learn the foxtrot but in fact you found yourself waltzing. Whatever you have learned or experienced and can now take with you, know that you are right where you are meant to be.

Thank you for joining our DANCE class. I hope it has been a rewarding, empowering, insightful and enjoyable experience. For some of you, it may have been life-altering. For others, it may have been a step in a new direction – your true direction. Either way, what you do with your dance now is up to you. Claim it! Own it! Live it!

Our life patterns and habits have been built on years of decision making and action choices. These patterns will not change overnight. It takes only 7 days to start a new habit and at least 21 days to end an old habit. Be patient with yourself as you continue on your DANCE journey. I appreciate the opportunity to have shared the dance floor with you.

Hopefully, this life metaphor of the DANCE will be a powerful reminder for the choices that lie before you every day! Your decisions have all the power to potentially lead you toward peace, contentment and happiness. Your authentic life!

When your choices are right before you on the dance floor of life and you have the decision to sit it out or dance, I hope you DANCE!

DANCE! DANCE! DANCE!

Deborah's Recommended List of Readings to Strengthen the Components of Your DANCE Floor

Over the course of the years, a variety of sources have strengthened my perspective of life and enduring happiness. Here are some of the books that were most influential and are worth considering.

Augustine, S. (1997). *With wings there are no barriers: A Womans' guide to a life of magnificent possibilities*. Louisiana: Pelican Publishing Company, Inc.

Austin, L. (2000). *What's holding you back?* New York, NY: Basic Books.

Ban Breathnach, S. (1995). *Simple abundance: A daybook of comfort and joy*. New York, NY: Warner Books, Inc.

Bender, P.U. (2002). *Gutfeeling*. Toronto, ON: The Achievement Group.

Boothman, N. (2000). *How to make people like you in 90 seconds or less*. New York, NY: Workman Publishing Company, Inc.

Coloroso, B. (1995) *Kids Are Worth It!* Toronto, ON: Somerville House Publishing.

Carlson, R. & Shield, B. (Eds.) (1995). *Handbook for the soul*. Canada: Little, Brown & Company (Canada) Ltd.

Chopra, D. (1997). *The path to love: Spiritual strategies for healing*. NewYork, NY: Three Rivers Press.

Covey, S. (1997). *The 7 Habits of highly effective families*. NewYork, NY: Franklin Covey Company.

Dyer. W. (1997). *Manifest your destiny: The nine spiritual principles for getting everything you want.* New York, NY: Harper Collins Publishers.

Erikson, E. H. (1980). *Identity and the Life Cycle.* New York, NY: W. W. Norton & Company.

Freston, K. (2003). *Expect a Miracle: 7 Spiritual steps to finding the right relationship.* New York, NY, St. Martin's Press.

Glover Scott, K. (2000). *Esteem: A powerful guide to building the self-esteem you want and the life you deserve.* Ingersoll, ON: Alternative Truths Press.

Gray, J. (1992). *Men are from Mars, Women are from Venus.* New York, NY: J. G. Productions, Inc.

Heavin, G. and Colman,C. (2003). *Curves: Permanent Results without Permanent Dieting.* New York, NY: G.P. Putman's Sons.

McKay, G. and Dinkmeyer, D. (1994). *How you feel is up to you: The power of emotional choice.* San Luis Obispo, CA: Impact Publishers, Inc.

Quotes & Quips: Insights on Living the 7 Habits. (1998). Salt Lake City, Utah: Franklin Covey Co.

Richardson, C. (1999). *Take time for your life.* New York, NY: Broadway Books.

Ripplinger-Fenwick, C. (1995). *Healing with humour: A laughter first-aid kit.* Muenster, SK: St. Peter's Press.

Robbins, A. (1991). *Awaken the giant within.* New York, NY: Fireside Books.

Sharma, R. S. (1997). *The Monk who sold his Ferrari*. Toronto, ON: Harper Collins Canada.

Sher, B. (1995). *I could do anything if I only knew what it was*. New York, NY: Dell Publishing.

Singh, R. N. (1996). *Self healing: Powerful techniques*. London, ON: Health Psychology Associates Inc.

Vanzant, I. (1998). *In the Meantime: Finding yourself and the love you want*. New York, NY: Simon & Schuster.

Warren, Neil Clark (1997). *Finding Contentment*. Nashville, TE; Thomas Nelson Publishers.

Young, J. E. and Klosko, J. S., (1993). *Reinventing your life*. New York, NY: Penguin Books USA, Inc.

Workshops, Keynotes and Seminars

-to inspire!
-to inform!
-to motivate your audience to live their best life!

Including: Stress management
Life balance
Communication
Relationship Building
Emotional Health
Parenting Issues and more...

To book Deborah DeJong for a workshop, seminar or speaking engagement or to receive more information about the many professional and personalized topics she addresses, please call (519) 503-5883 or visit www.innervoice.ca.

About the Author

Deborah DeJong, BA, MSW, has spent the last 15 years in the human services field working in the educational, correctional, and medical setting as well as children's and adult mental health agencies. As a trainer, facilitator and professional speaker, she has been empowering individuals, families and groups to live *their* best life!

She received her Master of Social Work from Wilfrid Laurier University, Waterloo (1992) and her Bachelor of Arts from Renison College, University of Waterloo (1990). She is a Director of Training and is dedicated to sharing the fundamental lessons that will empower people to move forward personally and professionally. She is a celebrated speaker and a regular guest on local television programming.

We hope you have enjoyed reading
DANCE: *Five Steps to Living Your Best Life.*

Could a friend or collegue benefit
from the DANCE?

If you would like to order additional copies,
please visit www.innervoice.ca on the internet.

You may also order by sending a cheque or
money order to:
Inner Voice
5-420 Erb Street W., Suite 434, Waterloo ON N2L 6K6

Name: _____

Address: _____

_____

_____

Postal Code: _____

Telephone Number: _____

Number of copies _____
@ 18.95 CDN or 14.95 USD = $ _____

Add GST @7%
    (Canadian residents only) = $ _____

Add shipping and handling:
    $4.00 for one book +
    $1.00 for each additional
    book to a maximum of $10.00 = $ _____

                              Total = $ _____

(US orders, please submit in US funds)

VISA or Mastercard orders are also accepted.

Card number _____

Exp. date _____

Signature _____
Your book(s) will be sent by post. Please allow 2-3 weeks for delivery.